The Celestial Nāgasvaram

Classical Musical Instruments from India, no. 2

The Celestial Nāgasvaram

Origin, Myths, Reception and the Maestros

Geetha Rajagopal

with a Foreword by

Veena E. Gayathri

Publishers

First published in India in 2015

Cataloging in Publication Data--DK
[Courtesy: D.K. Agencies (P) Ltd. <docinfo@dkagencies.com>]

Rajagopal, Geetha, 1948-
The celestial nāgasvaram : origin, myths, reception and the maestros / Geetha Rajagopal ; with a foreword by Veena E. Gayathri .
p. cm. – (Classical musical instruments from India ; no. 2)
Includes bibliographical references (p.).
ISBN: 978-81-927021-2-4

1. Nāgasvaram music – India, South – History and criticism. I. Title. II. Series: Classical musical instruments from India ; no. 2.

DDC 788.9909548 23

Cover design: Jyothi Menon
Photographs: Ashwin Rajagopal and Geetha Rajagopal

Published by:
Avi Publishers
Publishing with Rhythm
A-18, Mohan Garden
Near Nawada Metro Station
New Delhi–110 059
Phone: 011-2537-1324
e-mail: info@avipublishers.com
Web: www.avipublishers.com

Printed at: Salasar Imaging Systems, Delhi – 110 035

I dedicate this book to

My father, late Shri S.R. Srinivasan
— a voracious reader and writer —
who encouraged me from my childhood
to write on art and appreciate art;

My mother and my Guru
late Smt. Sakuntala Srinivasan
who trained me in Carnatic music
and to take up to research level;

My mother-in-law,
Smt. Vedavalli Srinivasan,
who supported me and encouraged me
in each and every endeavour;

And to my husband
Shri K.S. Rajagopalan, and my family
without whose support
this book would not have been possible.

Foreword

THE author of this book, Mrs Geetha Rajagopal is the director of SAMPRADAYA, a centre for south Indian music tradition.

The book, *The Celestial Nāgasvaram* penned by Mrs Geetha is about the traditional wind instrument of Tamil Nadu, the *nāgasvaram*. *Nāgasvaram* is basically a temple instrument. There are no temple festivals or auspicious events held without the *maṅgala vādyam,* i.e. *nāgasvaram*. This book elaborately deals with *nāgasvaram* the instrument; the playing techniques involved and also about the eminent *vidvān*s who played the instrument and added glory to it. The author has also written in detail about the Sangeetha Kalanidhi awardees among the *nāgasvaram vidvān*s. There are several colourful and rare photographs which enhance the uniqueness of this book.

I wish the author great success in all her endeavours.

E. Gayathri

Kalaimamani Veena E. Gayathri

Vice-Chancellor
Tamil Nadu Music and
Fine Arts University
Chennai - 600 028

Preface

NĀDA (sound vibration) is that which is pleasant to the ears (*karṇa*). *Laya* (rhythm or beat) is the very pulse of every movement in the universe. The little interlude between one sound to the other sound and one "vibration" to another is *laya*. There can be no *nāda* without *laya*, and no *laya* without *nāda*. Music is the language of gods and the language of emotions.

Going by the Hindu mythology, music and gods have an eternal relationship. Most of the Hindu gods are associated with a particular instrument — Lord Śiva (*ḍamaru*), Lord Kṛṣṇa (flute), Goddess Sarasvatī (*vīṇā*), Sage Nārada (*tānapūrā*), Nandī (god of percussion (*mṛdaṅgam*)) and so on.

Our forefathers understood the importance of absolute music and instilled in us the concept of association of musical instruments with gods and goddesses. Music is an integral part of India's religion and culture. It is styled by Gāndharva Veda (which is one among the four Upavedas), the other three being Dhanurveda (archery), Āyurveda (medicine), and Arthaśāstra (statecraft, economic policy and military policy).

The backbone of Indian life is religion. Spirituality is the life-blood of this sacred land and this is our most valued and precious inheritance. Temples and worship places manifest an unseen power. God's manifestation in the idol is the basis of our religious worship. Therefore, visits to such holy and sacred places have been our tradition, and that is being followed even today. The holy visits are conducted with utmost humility, purity in thought, word and deed.

Keeping this in mind our forefathers had set up time-honoured traditions, customs and tenets in the form of meditation, *bhajanas*, *nāmasaṅkīrtanas*, *satsaṅgas*, reading of sacred books, etc. These rituals were prescribed to us hundreds of years ago, with the sole purpose that an ardent devotee and an earnest seeker should feel the presence of the Omnipresent and derive spirituality through them.

From the time of Vedas and during the periods of Āgamas, Purāṇas and Itihāsas (ancient texts and literature), the Bhakti movement got spread all over India. It became very powerful during the medieval times.

God can be realized in many ways but *saṅgīta-mārga* (the path of music) is perhaps the easiest and the most pleasant way to reach Him. In south India, particularly in Tamil Nadu, the "Vaiṣṇavite" and the "Śaivite" mystics (the twelve Āḷvārs and the sixty-three Nāyanmārs, and great teachers like Rāmānujācārya, Śaṅkarācārya and Madhvācārya) and others took the new manifestation of spiritual force to dizzying heights through their spiritual hymns. The tremendous tidal waves rocked the other parts of the country, in the form of saints like Caitanya, Tukārām, Purandaradāsa, Tulasīdās, Sūrdās, Kabīr, Mīrābāī and many others.

Nāḷāyira Divya Prabandham, dedicated to Lord Viṣṇu, consists of 4,000 divine hymns composed by the twelve Āḷvārs and *Thirumurai* consists of the divine hymns dedicated to Lord Śiva by the sixty-three Nāyanmārs. These poets of the Bhakti period were inspirational and musically oriented to cater to the aesthetic senses of the common devotee.

It should be remembered that the Indian music and dance even influenced South-East Asia, particularly the island of Bali. While some of them recognized the curative and therapeutic power of music, the Indians also realized the spiritual power of music.

There is a popular saying in Sanskrit about music: *śruti-mātā-pītā-laya* — *śruti* (pitch) is the mother and *laya* (rhythm) is the father. Many of the deities have their own instruments and have always been worshipped as the embodiments of music or art. Lord Śiva is the embodiment of *nāda* eternally, playing *ḍamaru* and He is also the performer of *tāṇḍava* (celestial cosmic dance). Lord Brahmā is the origin of music inspired by *Sāmaveda*. From the word *oṁ* (*praṇava mantra*) the following concepts were emanated.

In his song *Nādatanumaniṣam* in Cittarañjanī Rāga, Tyāgarāja pays obeisance to Lord Śaṅkara, the embodiment of *nāda*, the primeval sound, to Him who delights in the seven notes — *Sā Re Gā Mā Pā Dhā Ni.* Born of His five faces are Sadyojātam, Vāmadevam, Tatpuruṣam, Īśanam and Aghoram. These five factors are identified as the five faces of Lord Śiva and it is believed that the musical notes have emanated from them and passed on to posterity. Lord Śiva was supposed to have taught this to his prime disciple and consort Pārvatī and from then on it was passed on to his other disciples — Sage Nārada, Tumburu, Goddess Sarasvatī, the eternal Vaiṅka and Nandikeśvara (the percussive, *mr̥daṅgam* exponent).

Goddess Sarasvatī (the goddess of knowledge) is always associated with *vīṇā*. Lord Kr̥ṣṇa, the eternal flautist, also claims that He is *Sāmaveda* among the Vedas. Goddess Pārvatī is the embodiment of *lāsya*. Lord Viṣṇu and His consort Goddess Lakṣmī (the goddess of wealth) are connoisseurs of music.

Sage Nārada is always associated with his *tānapūrā* and he is also known as the *vaiṇika gāyaka* (an exponent both in *vīṇā* and vocal music). Nandī, the bull, is the master of *laya* and is always associated with *mr̥daṅgam*. Demi-gods like *gandharva*s, *yakṣa*s and *kinnara*s were supposed to have been proficient in music and musical instruments.

There has always been a perfect unison of *nāda* and *laya* with *Paramātmā* (Supreme Power). Music and dance were never conceived as mere items of entertainment and in this unison one can find the "transcendental power" of *nādopāsanā*.

Classical music and dance had a natural place in with the Hindu temples and religion. Not only were their themes almost always religious, but the performances of dance and music were carried on in the temple premises where these were free for the public. The implication is that those who came to the temple, at least while they were within the temple, were in an elevated state of mind and did not look for cheap entertainment.

Several rulers (kings) in south India were patrons of the fine arts and artists. They built many fine temples in those days. We must remember that in those days temples served the same purpose as the modern auditoriums and patronized artists of different art forms.

Traditionally a balance was struck between the king, who ruled like a feudal lord and patron, and the power of religion. All arts and sciences prospered under the wings of the temples generously supported by the king.

On the other hand, the king's holy mission — to be victorious, respected and revered by his subjects, and maintain peace and calm within his own country — enhances rain and crops, was sustained by the temple priests who served both in temples and the royal court. In short, the temple priests were in-charge of the welfare of the subjects in every aspect.

Temples in south India have played a pivotal and predominant role in the development and preservation of music in its various forms. In India music and dance were never conceived as mere items of entertainment but as a means of salvation (*mokṣa*). Even the greatest men and women of the land treated music and dance as subjects worthy of serious study and practice.

The two main art forms — dance and music — were elevated to the status of *vidyā* (knowledge). They helped the intellect within men and women to understand and absorb something of the infinite.

Music for the Indians has always been the resource, from which they always seek comfort or solace in joy or grief, for prayer or praise. This shows why the Indians give so much of importance to music and why they have a religious passion for the fine arts. It also shows why the fine arts have religion as their very centre of soul and spirit.

In fact, it gives an insight into the important roles the temples played promoting and sustaining art forms, and how art and religion were incorporated into each other in every activity in some form or the other.

Music is a holy art in India. The spiritual side of music has taken deep roots in our land as the people have all along been more prone to spirituality. It is primarily because of the spiritual influence of the temples.

South India is a land of temples and every village invariably has a temple. In fact, the temple is the centre, around which the village is developed. These temples have not only been functioning as places of worship but also as centres of fine arts.

These art forms grew adjuncts to religion and the temples with their vast endowments had a regular establishment with artists like singers, dancers, accompanists (instruments), and composers for offering musical service in its essential precincts. The abundant epigraphical and inscriptional evidences bear testimony to all these fine arts. The hymns that have been preserved over the years also bear testimony to these fine arts. Thus all forms of music and dance became indispensable items of worship and rituals in the temples of south India.

South India has the unique distinction of having set its heart and soul on art and culture. There are no parallels to the hundreds of temples, sculptures and the art forms, and those activities related to these art forms.

It is also very interesting to note that almost all the big and ancient temples are found near rivers like Kāverī, Godāvarī, Tuṅgabhadrā and others. It seems as if even these holy rivers nurtured music and have been patrons to these fine arts.

Music became a way of life and at times mandatory for auspicious occasions like temple festivals, and religious, social, cultural and even political functions.

Temples and *maṭha*s were the bastions of cultural centres for the sustenance of musicians and propagation of music. Patronage was primarily the duty of royalty, while many affluent families took patronage of musicians as a status symbol.

Hence in this kind of atmosphere and ambience the artists gave their full to art which they considered divine. They performed as devotees offering their art to the Almighty. Great artists of the past had believed in *niṣkāma karma* (service without expectation and ego).

The rich heritage of musical traditions, that these great artists have left as a legacy to us, should be preserved for posterity keeping in mind that it is a way of enlightenment to realize the Supreme Bliss.

Contents

Acknowledgement

At the outset I would like to acknowledge the Sampradaya Archives and Library, a treasure house of research materials in south Indian music traditions, from which a lot of information has been collected.

I also would like to place on record my gratitude and thanks to all the family members of the Semponnarkoil Nagaswara Parampara who supported and encouraged me to bring out this book.

My heartfelt thanks to the great *nāgasvaraṃ* maestro Shri Semponnarkoil S.R. Rajanna who has been more like a *guru* to me and had been guiding me right through this project. I would also like to acknowledge my sincere thanks and appreciation to the following persons for their guidance and unconditional support.

1. Shri Ambalapuzha Shri Kumar Panicker, son of Gopalakrishna Panicker, Ambalapuzha (Brothers), Kerala.
2. Dr M.A. Bhageerathy, Head of the Music and Research Department, Queen Mary's College, Chennai.
3. Late Shri Chidamabaram Radhakrishna Pillai (*nāgasvaram* maestro).
4. Shri T.P. Girivasan (*mukha-vīṇā* maestro).
5. Late Shri T. Govindaraj Pillai (*nāgasvaram* maestro).
6. Shri S.R. Gurmurthy, son of Sri Semponnarkoil S.R. Rajanna Pillai.

7. Semponnarkoil Shri S.R. Rajanna.
8. Shri Raghuveeran, son of late *nāgasvaram* maestro Sri Sivasubramania Pillai.
9. Shri N.I.S. Kannan Acharya (*nāgasvaram* maker), Narasinganpettai Tanjavur district.
10. Shri S. Kumaravelu.
11. Shri S. Kumaravelu, State Bank of Travancore, Alappuzha.
12. Shri Leena Manohar Reddy, vocalist and musicolgist, Chitoor, Andhra Pradesh.
13. Late Shri T. Latchappa Pillai (*nāgasvaram* maestro).
14. Shri V. Murugadoss, *nāgasvaram* artist and Head of the Department, Kstera Kalapeetam, Vaikom, Kerala.
15. Shri S. Parthasarathy, percussionist and grandson of Shri Semponnarkoil S.R. Rajanna (*nāgasvaram* maestro).
16. Shri R.V. Sadasivan, Thripunithra, Kerala.
17. Shri Semponnarkoil S.R. Rajanna Pillai.
18. Shri Ramadasappa, Bangalore (*nāgasvaram* maestro).
19. Shri P.V.K. Sreedhar, Myladuthurai (Seevali-maker), Tanjavur district.
20. Shri B.M. Sundaram, musicologist and percussionist.

List of Figures

Introduction
Music Is a Form of Worship

MUSIC is equated with worship and *sādhanā* (spiritual practice). Music is the finest of all fine arts. It is also *vidyā* (knowledge). That is why in the earlier days it was called Upaveda, that which helps to realize the Supreme Being.

Temples have served as the nerve centre of the divine arts and prescribed to us as (1) *gītam* (music), (2) *vādyam* (instruments), and (3) *nṛtyam* (dance). These are essential parts of services (rituals).

Music is the best therapy for any ailment — physical or mental. Singing the hymns of God is the most effective remedy for all ailments of the human body and soul.

Saint Tyāgarāja in His Song

"Nāda Loludai Brahmanda", in the Kalyāṇa Vasanta Rāga, sings attain yourself the eternal bliss by immersing yourself in *nāda* as all the gods and great sages followed this.

Music is claimed to possess the power to "purify him that chants him and him that listens". Congregational musical recital of God's name helps even the inanimate, immovable and inert objects of God's creation to get imprints of the name of God by ethereal vibrations that in due time will bring liberation to them also.

Temples are like beacon lights and they lure people to come and taste the nectar of divine bliss. In Tamil there is a saying "that a town without a temple is unsuitable for habitation". The Saṅgam age poetess Auvvayār has quoted in *Athi Choodi,* a collection of poems for children:

> *kovil illadha ūril kudi iruka vendām* ।
> *ālayam tholuvadu salavum nanru* ॥
>
> Do not reside in a town where there is no temple.
> Worshipping in a temple is extremely virtuous.

Temples were designed to create environments congenial to the expansion of one's mind, soul and, above and beyond, the drab realities of life. They were constructed and equipped with the best reassures of all fine arts.

From *Kāmikāgama* one can see that the performance of music and dance was not something optional but an integral and compulsory part of rituals in worship. Temples have thus been the home of static dance and dynamic music.

Great ritual care is taken to keep alive all the divine forces embedded in the temple area peaceful and content. Like a royal Lord, the Divine Lord holds the court, receives visitors, listens to their requests, is awoken to the auspicious sounds of music, is bathed, dressed and fed, entertained and made to sleep (all through with music as the medium).

What is important is the belief and faith that God is emotionally involved with his devotees throughout the music rituals. One such art that took a gigantic form several centuries ago to establish itself in the temples and merge with the various religious rituals was *nāgasvaram*.

This evolution did not happen overnight but was like a renaissance that took its strides slowly, steadily and positively to stay on forever till eternity. The temples of south India, particularly in Tamil Nadu, stand as silent witnesses to this transformation from the silence to the voluminous sound *nāda* of *nāgasvaram* that has been going on ever since.

When one tries to bring in a picture of a particular temple or deity in one's mind, one picturizes not only the deity, but gets a whiff of the fragrance of the flowers and the incense, and above all the sweet sound of *nāgasvaram* that travels with him for a long distance, yearning him for the next trip.

Such is the power of *nāgasvaram* otherwise known as the *maṅgala-vādyam* (auspicious instrument) and also the *rāja vādyam* (king of all instruments).

To get to know more about *nāgasvaram,* one has to go deep into the history of the Thiruvarur Temple. The history of the temple connects us to the history of the dynasties — beginning with the Pallavas, to Chozhas (Coḷas), Pāṇḍyas and, later briefly, to Tanjavur Nāyakas and Marāṭhās.

The Thiruvarur Temple

"To be born in Thiruvarur is *mukti* (salvation) and to die in Benares is *mukti*" is an age-old saying.

The antiquity of the Thiruvarur Temple predates the documented history that begins with King Mahendra Pallava. This temple has served as an icon of Tamil Nadu for several centuries since the period of the Pallavas.

The poet Thirunavukarasu (one of the sixty-three Nāyanmārs) reveals in his poem about the rituals that were observed during the months of Marghazhi (December–anuary), Panguni (March–pril), Chitirai (April) and so on. These rituals were observed to please the presiding deity Lord Tyāgeśa and His consort Nīlotpalāmbal. All these existed before the rule of the Pallavas (seventh century CE), i.e. as early as the (sixth century CE).

The poet Appār (one of the sixty-three Nāyanmārs) had

dedicated twenty-one beautiful hymns to the presiding deity in the sixth century CE during the reign of Mahendra Pallava.

The temple was first re-built by Āditya Chozha in the seventh century CE and later a lot of additions were made by the other Chozha kings up to the tenth century CE.

The presence of rare musical instruments, dancers in various poses inscribed in copper plates, bronze plates, the sixty-five stone inscriptions and the historical ambiguity of the beautiful temple car, and other sculptures makes this temple as the "largest repository of Tamil cultural values and traditions".

The poet Sekkizhar was a minister in the royal court of Rājarāja Chozha. He authored the famous *Periya Purāṇam.* He was a staunch Śaivite and resigned his minister's post and became a devout Śaiva devotee serving Lord Tyāgeśa. One chapter in his *Periya Purāṇam* is dedicated to the temple and the deity, and gives all the details of the temple along with the traditions and rituals that were observed during his period.

Some of these details may be from the mythological stories interwoven with the history of the temple while some are references he has compiled from the poems of the Nāyanmārs. These lead us to a lot of information about the History of *nāgasvaram.*

1

Nāgasvaram
A Brief History

LIKE the Thiruvarur Temple (*fig.* 1) there are a lot of hidden mysteries or myths about *nāgasvaram* as there are different versions on its origin. This makes us to put the clock a little backwards to trace the origin of instrumental music. This by itself makes a very interesting study and leads us to the origin of *nāgasvaram* by navigating us through a long but exciting journey.

Instrumental music came to have a remarkable development with the emergence of the concept of *sukhabhāva saṅgīta* (melodious music) and absolute music. When we look into the cultural background of India, there has always been a period in which the arts have flourished and reached great heights of excellence, a period we commonly refer as the "golden age".

One such art form is *nāgasvaram,* a wind instrument that began its journey about 800 years ago from Thiruvarur, and slowly and steadily spread to the entire southern peninsula. It reached its zenith in the eighteenth century and the next 150 years saw this art in its most glorious and divine form.

Almost till the late 1960s this art enjoyed the status of the "golden age" and the *nāgasvaram* artists contributed their might to the rich cultural heritage of south India. More so because of the status the instrument enjoyed in the religious rituals of temples in particular and the society in general.

South India has a rich variety of musical instruments, both the classical and folk types. *Vīṇā, mṛdaṅgam* and *nāgasvaram* are instruments with highly evolved techniques. Centuries of evolution must have preceded their techniques before they reached the perfection.

Many instruments are referred in mythological stories and in the sacred hymns. Some of these instruments like *kuzhal* (flute) and *idakkai, berigai, parai, takkai, tālam* and *muzhavu* (all percussion instruments) are categorically mentioned in *Tevaram* hymns.

A verse quoted in Adiyarkkunallar's commentary contains a very long list of the above instruments (Tamil poem *Tevaram*):

berigai, padagam, idakkai, udukkai,
maddaḷam, salligai, karadigai, thimilai
damurugam, thannumai, thavil, thadaari,
ubaṅgam, thud iperumpaarai (ena)
*mikka nallor virith uraithanare**

The above verse in Tamil quoting names of most of the percussive instruments played by artists in temples is from the Tamil literary masterpiece of the Saṅgam Age *Śilappadikāram*.

Most of these instruments have survived to this day and have fortunately found their way into temples where they are found in sculptures, displayed in the temple archives or museums and some even played only during special occasions.

---

* The first four lines list the names of percussive instruments in Tamil. The last line says that these instruments were recognized and recommended by the learned men to be performed for gods.

Some of the above percussion instruments have had a permanent place in the ritualistic routine. It would be interesting to know that all these instruments are found in the "Vitaṅka Kṣetras".

The Vitaṅka Kṣetras are seven in number and they are: Thiruvarur, Thiruvaimur, Tirukkolili, Tirukkaravasaḷ, Tirunagaikaronam, Tirunallaru and Tirumaraikkaḍu. All these temples are in Tanjavur district.

In all the above-mentioned seven temples Lord Tyāgarāja is the presiding deity and, like Lord Naṭarāja, is associated with dance. This then explains the priority of the percussion instruments followed by *nāgasvaram* and other instruments for which they are used as accompaniments.

The Thiruvarur Temple in its *Sthala Purāṇam* (recorded temple history) details about the presiding deity, his consort, the temple tanks, *sthala vṛkṣa,* the daily rituals to be conducted, the festivals to be observed, and the eleven important factors that the deity is identified with.

Some of them are His: flag (Tyāgeśa *koḍi*), sword (*vīra-kāṇḍayam*), dance (*ajaba*), seat (ruby-studded), animal (*iravadam* — elephant), instrument (*bāri nayanam*), percussion (*śuddha maddalam*), beats or steps (*pañca-mukha vādyam*) and carriage (horse). So, on record, we find the name *bāri nayanam* (*nāgasvaram* is also known as *nayanam*) that has been played or dedicated to the deity.

Lord Tyāgeśa is known as Rājātirāja (king of kings) and a convoy that accompanied was mandatory with the following: the head priest, Śaivite savants, scholars, dancers, singers, other musicians, devotees, elephants, horses (cavalry, infantry), etc.

This again shows how traditions were followed everyday in every activity and were prescribed centuries ago. It also gives a very colourful vision of a magnificent pageant that might have taken place everyday with so many musicians playing their instruments and following the Lord every time He made His entry into the town to visit His devotees.

From time immemorial India possesses a rich variety of musical nstruments. Almost all types of instruments classified as wind, stringed and percussions have been played in temples and references are available in literature and temples (inscriptions and sculptures). Many Hindu gods and goddesses are associated with some instruments like Lord Kṛṣṇa (flute), Lord Śiva (*ḍamaru*), Goddess Sarasvatī (*vīṇā*), Sage Nārada (*tānapūrā*), Nandī (the god of percussion (*mṛdaṅgam*)) and so on.

Several musical instruments are referred to in the Saṅgam literature of the Tamils, dating back to the second century CE. The *kombu* and *ekkalam* are instruments referred in the Saṅgam literature, and these are wind instruments. Both these instruments were played at temples and palaces, and on the occasion of festivals. They were mainly played to announce or herald the arrival of God's or king's visit outside the temple/palace so people could be prepared to receive them formally and offer their homage. These were also meant to be used during war times to alert or caution people of the insurgence of enemies (like a siren that was used during war times).

They were not instruments that were played as an accompaniment like the *yazh* (harp), *vīṇā* or *kuzhal* (flute), but were just blown to their full volume that sounded like the trumpeting of the elephant.

Ekkalam (*fig.* 2a, b) looks somewhat like a huge *nāgasvaram* (a trumpet). The flute known as *vaṅgiyam* or *kuzhal* was the most popular wind instrument and was found in various kinds and forms. There were also different forms of trumpets like *kombu* and *śaṅkha. Vaṅgiyam* was also known as *ezhil,* meaning one with seven holes (*nāgasvaram* also has seven holes).

Nāgasvaram was not mentioned in the Saṅgam literature and scholars opine that it must have been of a later origin. This exclusive instrument of Tamil Nadu has a glorious tradition of 800 years behind it. Built by great rulers, kings and a galaxy of stalwarts, *nāgasvaram* is perhaps the most vastly heard musical instrument in south India.

There is hardly another musical culture in the world that is as intensive and audible as Indian classical music. It leads the listener into an absolute silence of spiritual realization. We can hear *nāgasvaram* in almost all the temples — religious functions, festivals and weddings. It is used as an accompaniment for folk music and other folk art forms like street plays and folk dances, where it is a part of a band known as *nayandi melam.*

In this band the *nāgasvaram* artist sometimes dances and plays to the beat of the percussive instruments. Again *nāgasvaram* here is only used in plays or dances that narrate stories from the epics more like folklore, set to folk tunes. As it is considered as an instrument that is played for all auspicious occasions it became mandatory to play *nāgasvaram* on all religious occasions.

Hence there is no dearth of *nāgasvaram* players and the temple establishments have an assured place for them. Known as *maṅgala-vādyam* (auspicious instrument) its very sound is indicative of a joyous occasion. It is the principal outdoor instrument and can be heard from long distances, especially during early mornings and nights.

It is no exaggeration to say that *nāgasvaram* has vastly contributed to the development of south Indian culture, traditions and fine arts. It is an integral part of temple festivals, marriages, and all religious functions and auspicious occasions.

Musicologists and scholars are of the opinion that *nāgasvaram* is a bigger version of the instrument referred as *peruvaṅgiyam* and *nedu vaṅgiyam* in ancient Tamil literature *Śilappadikāram*. *Peru* means big in Tamil and *vaṅgiyam* means flute. The big here refers to the volume of the instrument and *nedu* means long instrument.

Musicologists suggest that *nāgasvaram* is not more than 800 years old. It is not seen in the very old and important temple sculptures. Neither do we find any reference to the instrument in *Kāmikāgama,* the literary work dealing with temples and temple rituals. From it we get the information about instruments that had to be played or were prescribed for the *navasandhi* rituals (music and dance rituals) performed in different directions like east, west, north and south while the deity was taken around the temple. It is also not mentioned in *Saṅgīta Ratnākara* written in the early thirteenth century or in *Kamba Rāmāyaṇa.*

Mukha-vīṇā (*fig.* 3), a smaller version of *nāgasvaram,* is referred to in *Saṅgīta Ratnākara* — and *nāgasvaram* is a bigger or modified version of it according to many musicologists.

Nāgasvaram or Nādasvaram?

The instrument *bhujaṅgasvaram,* also known as *maguḍi* (it is the instrument that is played by the snake charmers and known as *bīna* in north India), is referred in *Saṅgīta Ratnākara.* There is a sculpture of a performer playing *maguḍi* and a serpent dancing in front of him in the temple at Thirukazhundram in Chinglepet district, about 65 km from Chennai.

When *nāgasvaram* emerged, its tone was found to very much resembling to that of *bhujaṅgasvaram.* Hence it came to be called *nāgasvaram* to distinguish it from the snake charmer's instrument — *bhujaṅga* and *nāga* both meaning serpent. The instrument also gives an appearance of a snake when seen from upwards to downwards.

There is also a lot of disagreements among musicologists about the correct name of the instrument and *nāgasvaram* artists claim that the correct name is *nādasvaram* and some calling it *nādasvaram*. *Nāda,* denotes sound and *svara* notes, implying the meaning "sound that creates notes". It is also known as *nayanam* and *nāgacinnam.*

A majority of performers and musicologists claim that the right word is *nāgasvaram*. Ahobala in his *Saṅgīta Pārijāta* separately describes *nāgasvaram* and *mukha-vīṇā*. The word *nāgasvaram* gained popularity amongst performers only during the early eighteenth century.

The great composer Sri Muthuswamy Dikshitar has composed a *kr̥ti* (composition) in Śrīrāgam in praise of the presiding deity Lord Tyāgarājaswāmy at Thiruvarur. The composer's father had formatted several *nāgasvara* rituals for the Thiruvarur Temple and the particular *nāgasvaram* in Thiruvarur is known as *bāri nayanam*. It has been played only in this temple by the artists who have been there for several generations.

In *anu pallavī* (mid-portion) of the Śrīrāgam composition Dikshitar sings:

> *pallavī* (beginning) — *tyāgarāja mahadh vajaroha*
> *anupallavī — āgama siddhānta pratipādyam, nāgasvara maddaḷaivādam*

Lord Tyāgeśa is one who is accompanied by *nāgasvaram* and *maddaḷam.*

This verse has the instrument named as *nāgasvaram.* This has been widely accepted by several musicologists as authentic and hence they refer the instrument as *nāgasvaram.* One of the earliest references to *nāgasvaram* was found in the Telugu literary work of Śrī Vallabhācārya, *Krīḍābiramam*. Also the book titled *Narasiṁha Purāṇam* in Telugu by Sri Haribhaṭa, a contemporary of King Kṛṣṇadeva Rāya, mentions *nāgasvaram* along with other instruments.

According to eminent musicologist and *vaiṇika* Sri Ranga Ramanuja Iyengar, *nāgasvaram* was introduced by Nada Nayanar in the thirteenth century. He says *nāgasvaram* took for its companion *tavil*, well matched in majestic "sound and power".

Going with all these references we will have to accept the fact that *nāgasvaram* and *tavil* took their birth in the Thiruvarur Temple and later nurtured and fostered by other temples.

This art form slowly and steadily progressed within the four walls of the temples only to establish itself finally as an essential and integral part of rituals in the temple worship. Thus the two art forms — *nāgasvaram* (*nāda* — sound) and *tavil* (*laya* — rhythm) developed as one art form — made for each other and complimenting each other.

Nāgasvaram or *nādasvaram* was once upon a time the most heard musical instrument in south India, played in almost all temples, big or small, from 4.30 a.m. till about 9.30 p.m. everyday. It is no exaggeration to say that people were woken up by this instrument and slept to the sweet lullaby by it.

Nāgasvaram was pre-eminently an instrument meant for the open air, played for vast crowds for the happy solemnity of temple festivals, particularly those held outside the *sanctum sanctorum*. It is considered as the most auspicious (*maṅgala-vādyam*) and has become an integral part of all Hindu functions like weddings, *upanayanas* (thread ceremony), like cradling ceremony, birthday (first, sixty and eighty), inauguration of functions and, above all, temple festivals.

Even though *vīṇā* is a much older instrument, *nāgasvaram,* which is younger of the two, is given more importance. The reason: it depicts our culture and is synonymous with anything that is divine and auspicious. It is also known as *rāja vādyam* (king of all instruments).

Nāgasvaram: The Origin

Very little is known about the origin of *nāgasvaram.* However, there is a story associated with Emperor Rājarāja Chozha I. Shri T. Latchappa Pillai unveils that story of how *nāgasvaram* came to get the status it enjoys today and it is dated back about 800 years. During the reign of the Emperor Rājarāja Chozha I, there was a severe drought in Tanjavur. Those were the days when Rājarāja Chozha was believed to have visited the Thiruvarur Temple once a week through a secret tunnel (known as *suraṅga padai*) passage built underground leading from Tanjavur to Thiruvarur. The king performed many *pūjā*s and *yajña*s beseeching the rain-god Lord Varuṇa for rains. But it was all a waste as the rain-god did not heed to his prayers.

The emperor's chief minister suggested that the king should invite the *nāgasvaram* players from Thiruvarur to come and perform (pray) to the rain-god at the Tanjavur Palace. The *nāgasvaram* players from Thiruvarur Temple came the very next day to the Tanjavur Palace and performed for more than three hours. The emperor, who was mesmerized by the music, stepped out of the palace and was taken by surprise, seeing the torrential rains. He proclaimed:

> *Nāgasvaram* certainly has the power and divinity to evoke rains and hence from this very day should be played in all the existing temples and temples that would

be built in the years to come by me and the generations to come.

The emperor also made a proclamation that the *nāgasvaram* artists would be treated with utmost respect by one and all in the society and would be given a lot of benefits like land, houses and money permanently which would be followed even after his death by his successors. He also asked the minister to make playing of the instrument mandatory in all religious functions in and outside the temple because he felt that the instrument was symbolic with both divinity and auspiciousness.

To make sure it went on record, the emperor got all the conditions inscribed in prominent parts of the temple. We find such inscriptions in a number of temples built by the Chozha kings in and around Tanjavur (*figs.* 4-5) like Thiruvarur, Gaṅgaikoṇḍa Chozhapuram and Kumbakoṇam. The *nāgasvaram* artists are given the topmost priority in these inscriptions.

When the emperor wanted to give the players gifts, they asked him for a *nāgasvaram* made in ivory and gifted to them. It was promptly made and gifted to the players. The sculptors (*sthapati*s) in the palace also wanted to gift the *nāgasvaram* players something; so they made one *nāgasvaram* in stone and gifted to them. The ivory one is with Shri Latchappa Pillai and was displayed in our programme (*fig.* 6). "Saṁvāda" is a unique project. It is a dialogue featuring a stalwart in conversation with another musician. This conversation series is designed to provide a public platform to facilitate musicians/musicologists/ music students and music lovers to have a one-to-one interaction with veteran musicians. This is one such tête-à tête featuring *nāgasvaram* maestro late Shri Tiruvarur Latchappa Pillai with Dr M.A. Bhageerathy held on 24 October 2010 at Raga Sudha Hall, Mylapore, Chennai.

The above myths or stories related to *nāgasvaram* may be true or false. It may just be a belief or something passed on from one generation to the other. But fact remains that *nāgasvaram* is an instrument that is considered auspicious and given utmost importance and priority in all temples and auspicious functions like weddings and birthdays till today. It is also considered sacred as people believe that it was brought to the Thiruvarur Temple by God Himself.

That *nāgasvaram* originated from Thiruvarur there are no second thoughts. The tradition of playing the instrument in the temple and making it a ritual with set pattern originated only from Thiruvarur, are on records as evidence. According to historians, the Thiruvarur Temple is the oldest of all temples and the Hindus believe that it was built by the heavenly beings (*deva*s) and not by human beings (*mānuṣa*).

Dramas were presented in the temple on sacred themes such as "Alagar Kuravañji", "Tyāgeśa Kuravañji" and "Kumbheśvarar Kuravañji". These were noted for their fine music and were the representatives of the golden age of music. *Nāgasvaram* is a part of the above musical themes that were heard over long distances and heralded the sacredness of the temple and at the same time served to carry the thoughts towards the divine.

The copper-plate record of the eighth century CE which has been recently discovered from the Nāgeśvara Swāmi Temple at Kumbakoṇam, records a grant to the "Nāgapāśa" community towards the establishment of the "Periyamelam", "Chinna melam", Nattumuttu artists, etc. in the temple. This copper plate is highly valuable as more than thirty kinds of wind instruments are inscribed on it and most prominent among them are *nāgasvaram* and *ekkalam*.

At the Ādi Kumbheśvara Temple in Kumbakoṇam we find the oldest *nāgasvaram* made of stone kept at display (*fig.* 7). In the Shenbaganallur Temple in Tirunelveli district we find the musical pipe *ekkalam* carved on a granite pillar. When touched it gives the sound of both *ekkalam* and conch. Literary works like *Karaṇāgama* and *Mahābhārata Cūḍāmaṇi* mention various musical instruments used in temple music and *nāgasvaram* finds a prominent place in both these works.

In south India, *vīṇā*, flute and *nāgasvaram* have enjoyed a very prestigious position and are considered to be the divine musical instruments. Of these, *nāgasvaram* has a unique place being it an integral part of the temple and religious rituals.

Nāgasvaram is the only form of music that can be heard and enjoyed in an open air by thousands of people and owing to this it has become a significant instrument in the growth of the musical knowledge among the masses. Another speciality of *nāgasvaram* is that it is the only instrument that is often played all through the night in the temple festivals. As a result of this unique feature of this instrument, people have adapted themselves listening to the long sessions of *ālāpana*s and have developed a taste for classical music.

One noteworthy thing about the *nāgasvaram* artists is that most of them have their village or town names pre-fixed to their names even before their initials. When I say the names of villages or towns it means those villages or towns that are known for the famous temples they are identified with like the Semponnarkoil (*fig.* 8), Chidambaram, Alappuzha, Thiruveṅgaḍu, Thirupamburam and Thiruvaduthurai temples. The artists had always identified themselves with the temples or the *maṭha*s to which they were attached because they did not want an individual identity. They wanted recognition only through the temples or *maṭhas* to which they were attached and where they served as *āsthāna vidvāns*. In all, it is just the divine unison of the art, the temple and the artist.

The temples seem to convey just one message to us that these great-hearted torch bearers — the *nāgasvaram* players and *tavil* players — keep awake and standing for hours together, pouring celestial music to soothe our bodies and minds, exalt us to great heights of divine bliss.

P.S. Veeruswamy Pillai, a *nāgasvaram* maestro, in his keynote address at the Music Academy, on being conferred the *Saṅgīta Kalānidhi* in the year 1961, said:

> *Nāgasvaram* occupies an important place in the Carnatic music system. It has become an integral part of the temples. It is also the first adjunct to any auspicious function, festival or auspicious occasion in our society.
>
> It is an instrument giving full scope to imagination, improvisation and the display of the intricacies of rhythm. It is an instrument that does not need any amplifier.
>
> I am fortunate to have had close acquaintance and benefit of association of great stalwarts like Semponnarkoil Ramaswamy Pillai, Mannargudi Chinna Pakkiria Pillai, Madurai Ponnuswamy Pillai, Chidambaram Vaidyanatha Pillai, Thiruppamburam Brothers, T.N. Rajarathnam Pillai and others and have also had the good fortune to have played with all these great legends.

In his interview to *Sampradāya* the legendary vocalist Sri Semmangudi has said about his experiences in temple festivals where seven or eight pairs of *nāgasvaram vidvāns* would play *mallāri* at the temple festivals during the *gopura-vasal ārādhanā* (outside the entrance of the temple tower) and the *vīdhi purappadu* (taken out in the streets) together in unison. At such moments even an atheist would feel overwhelmed by *bhakti*.

Nāgasvaram and Its Journey

The late T. Latchappa Pillai, a great *nāgasvaram* maestro, belonged to a family of *nāgasvaram* players (according to him he belonged to the twenty-fifth generation) attached to the Thiruvarur Temple. He had given two exclusive interviews to *Sampradāya* once in December 1986 (in-house interview) and once again in April 2010 in the presence of a huge audience where he presented a lecture demonstration.

According to Pillai the Tiruvarur Temple is the oldest and the first temple that was built in south India. The presiding deity is believed to be *svayambhū*, i.e. it had appeared on its own. About the presiding deity, Appār describes the Lord thus in his hymn — *aruvamun uruvamum ānai* (you were first invisible but now you have made your presence felt by your appearance to your devotees).

In Sekkizhar's *Periya Purāṇam* there is a chapter "Tyāgeśa Purāṇam" in which we find information about the Thiruvarur Temple. Several centuries ago, a community known as "Nayanār Ādiyar" came and settled in Thiruvarur. The word *nayanār* means devotees of Śiva or devotees who serve Śiva. Probably the word *nāyanmār* originated from this word. According to him these people came with the presiding deity of Thiruvarur Śrī Tyāgarāja. They were supposed to have been the direct descendants of *devas*.

It is believed that when they came, they brought with them the instrument called *bāri* (*fig.* 9) and these artists since then began to play this instrument at the Thiruvarur Temple. These *bāri nayanam* players, otherwise known as Nayanār Ādiyar, are to this day known with this name and interestingly only in Thiruvarur.

Every year, for several centuries, the Tyāgeśa festival

began with the hoisting of the flag. All the artists who took part in the festival were called upon to receive their honours. Nayanār Āḍigaḷar have always been the first to be called upon to accept the honours from the time of King Rājarāja Chozha. He had made this ritual mandatory and had also gifted these *bāri nayanam* players with land, paddy, etc. To ensure that the monetary benefits and other benefits would continue for the *nāgasvaram* artists even after his time, the king placed all this on record on the temple walls in the form of inscriptions. This age-old tradition of calling them first to present the honours on the first day of the festival still continues. The *nāgasvaram* artists are still addressed as "Nayanār Āḍigaḷar" and receive the temple honours first from the temple authorities and only then the other rituals begin. The land that was given to them still bears the name Nayanār Ādiyar Madam and is near to the temple between *kīzh vīdhi* (lower street) and *therku vīdhi* (south street).

That was the time when a lot of *devadāsī*s, also called as *devara-adiyar*, were serving in the temple as musicians and dancers. The word *devara* means God and *adiyar* means one who serves. One of the main instruments used during that period for accompanying the dance was the *mukha-vīṇā*, a much smaller version of *bāri*.

Those were the days when dance and dancers (*devadāsī*s) enjoyed priority and prestigious positions in the temple. *Devadāsī*s used to conduct all the religious rituals and were in full command of all temple-related activities. Some of the king's ministers, religious heads, astrologers and advisors felt that *devadāsī*s were not pure enough to serve gods directly and advised that it should be done only by learned people like *paṇḍita*s who were scholars in scriptures and Vedas. This then brought a change in the temple scenario when *devadāsī*s were given the duty of service to gods through art, and the rituals began to take shape under the learned *paṇḍitas*.

Musical Instruments and Their Classification

Musical instruments have been in existence since the dawn of early history and making of musical instruments is considered to be one of the most ancient arts in the world. Perhaps we can say that it is one of the oldest professions in the world.

A study of the ancient musical instruments shows the evolution of the instrument that began from simple bow strings and time-keeping instruments (where two sticks were used) to complex instruments. These later developed slowly and attained perfection in playing techniques and kept pace with the development in music as it is today.

Metals (brass, bronze, copper, silver), gourds, bamboo, canes, reeds, wood (jackfruit wood, black-wood), earthenware, animal skin, etc. have been used in the making of instruments.

Of the stringed, wind and percussion instruments, the percussive varieties are the oldest and percussion group instruments are found in different states of India. The stringed instruments came much later and the last to come among them was the wind instrument.

CLASSIFICATION OF MUSICAL INSTRUMENTS

Percussion Group

1. Stone-gongs
2. Drums
3. Pot drums
4. Wooden drums with open frame covered with animal skin
5. Metallic cymbals
6. Drums that could be tuned to desired pitch

(*mr̥daṅgam,* etc.) which have complex drum heads.

Stringed Group

1. Bow string and harp
2. Primitive lute
3. *Ekatārā, tuntina* with resonators
4. *Svaramaṇḍala*
5. *Vīṇā* with movable frets
6. *Vīṇā* (with fixed frets) like *rudra-vīṇā, sarasvatī-vīṇā* and *goṭuvādyam*
7. Bowed varieties of advanced type that came later like violin and *sāraṅgī*
8. Mechanically struck varieties provided with a keyboard like harmonium, piano and harpsichord.
9. The remote ancestor of the piano according to some musicologists is *śata-tantrī vīṇā* of very ancient times played with the help of a little hammer.

Wind Group

1. The wind group comprises of horn, *kombu, ekkalam* and long musical pipes without finger holes.
2. Gourd pipes
3. Pan-pipes
4. Musical pipes with few finger holes
5. Musical pipes with seven or eight finger holes like flute
6. Musical pipes with mouthpieces like *nāgasvaram, mukha-vīṇā* and *shehnāī*
7. Later the wind instruments with keyboard like organ and harmonium, which are of the Western origin.

Wind instruments are either of the wood-wind type

— *nāgasvaram*, oboe, clarinet, etc. or the brass-wind type — *thiruchinnam, kombu* (metallic horn) a compound instrument provided with a drone pipe and a tune pipe. Wind instruments are again of two kinds. First, those instruments therein wind is supplied by some mechanical contrivance commonly known as bellows. Organ and harmonium belong to this category. The second kind of wind instrument is where the wind is supplied by the breath of the performer. In this variety we again have two categories — mouth blown and nose blown. The mouth blown is again further classified into two types:

1. Instruments that are blown through vibrating reeds, tongues or mouthpieces.
2. A type where the wind is blown through orifices lie in the wall of the instrument — flute for example.

Among the wind instruments, flute and *nāgasvaram* have finger holes and *ekkalam*, conch, *kombu*, *thiruchinnam* (all played in temples), etc. do not have finger holes.

Thus *nāgasvaram* belongs to the family of wood-wind instruments. It has the status of both temple music and concert music (enjoys the status of primary instrument). The sound is produced by the vibration of a column of air that comes from the tube. Like flute, *nāgasvaram* has a range of two-and-half octaves and also a similar system in fingering. But the similarity ends here. In flute, semi and quarter tones are produced by the partial opening and closing of the finger holes. In *nāgasvaram*, the quarter tones are produced by adjusting the pressure and the strength of the air flow into the pipe. This exercise needs a lot of stamina and makes the instrument very exerting and strenuous.

The other difference between *nāgasvaram* and flute is the volume — *nāgasvaram* due to its intense volume is rightly suited for open air performances unlike flute that is suitable only for auditoriums and indoors. We can say that *nāgasvaram* is the south Indian version of *shehnāī,* but substantially a larger version. *Nāgasvaram* is the world's loudest non-brass acoustic instrument. It has a hard wooden body and a large flaring bell, made of wood or metal.

Nāgasvaram Making

Making of *nāgasvaram* calls for high dexterity and the artisan with his well-acquired skill and dedication makes it (*figs.* 10-11). Many consider its making a pious work. *Nāgasvaram* is made using wood, stone and ivory. We have already seen that the artists from Thiruvarur, who were invited by the emperor to play at the Tanjavur Palace, were gifted with an ivory *nāgasvaram*. It was played only on special occasions. Some *nāgasvarams* were also made of soap-stone, known as steatite, gave a very good tone. One such *nāgasvaram* can be seen at the temple of Azhwarthirunagari in Tirunelveli district.

As a product, *nāgasvaram* is primarily made of a wooden conical bore which enlarges as it comes downwards. There are another components made of metal or ivory. The wood that is used to make *nāgasvaram* of ebony is known as *accamaram*. Its botanical name is *Diospyros ebenaster*. The mouthpiece of *nāgasvaram,* called *narukku* in Tamil is made out of a reed — known as *korukkai* (*korukkan thattai*) in Tamil. In olden days *nāgasvarams* were also made of sandalwood, red wood and at times even of silver.

Nāgasvaram has a double reed and not a complex quadruple reed. The tree from which the wood to make *nāgasvaram* is taken has to be at least 100 years old and seasoned properly. Though musical instruments are made in metals, ivory and stone, wood is preferred as the tonal quality of the instruments improves in the long usage when they are made in wood. The resonators of aerophonic instruments like *nāgasvaram*, *mukha-vīṇā,* oboe and clarinet are made of wood.

In a study it was found out that the resonant quality of jackwood grown in the vicinity of temples is superior to that of the wood grown elsewhere. This may be due to the fact that these trees growing in the ambience of temple music from instruments like *nāgasvaram* and conch, and have become musically responsive.

It is important that the seasoning of wood is done with utmost care and competence because:

- The seasoned wood gives good tone or sound.
- It helps to fix proper conditioning in the structure of the wood.
- Seasoning helps to keep away insects and vermin from harming the instrument in the long run.
- Seasoning helps to remove the innate moisture from the wood.

To find out the quality of seasoning of the wood, a little test is prescribed. When the stem of the tree is lit at the top, it should burn steadily like the wick of a lit oil lamp or the wick of a candle.

Nāgasvaram consists of three divisions or parts — *kuzhal, thimiru* and *anaisu*. *Mel-anaisu* is a small metallic cylinder at the top of the instrument. *Kendai* is introduced and into it a mouthpiece, known as *narukku,* is inserted. *Narukku* is commonly known as *sīvali* (mouthpiece) (see *figs.* 12-14). The final processing of *sīvali* is done only by the *nāgasvaram* artist who will play it.

Sīvali is made from a reed known in the Tamil language as *korukkai* also known as *korukkan tattai*. This is a kind of a grass that is generally found in the marshy places on the riverbanks. These reeds are cut to the required shape and pressed and seasoned for nearly a year before it is put to use. *Nāgasvaram* has seven finger-holes, besides which there are five other holes that are drilled at the bottom. These holes serve as controllers. Of the five holes there are two pairs of holes opposite to each other and one near the circumference. These are known as the *brahma svara*s. The fifth hole, lower down, is known as the *adahara sram* and serves as the exit for the surplus air.

A metallic bell, known as *kizh* (lower) *anaisu,* adorns the bottom of the instrument. Sometimes the top and the bottom are made of the same wood as that of the conical bore of the instrument. Besides spare reeds, a bodkin of ivory or horn, known as *gejjikali* is used to clear the mouthpiece of the lingering particles of saliva, sticking in the sides and blocking the free flow of air. This bodkin is called *kucci.*

A chain is used to connect the metal staple at the top and a bell at the bottom. The *nāgasvaram* artists attach medals received by them in recognition of their performance to this chain, making the instrument look very decorative and colourful.

Some of the artisans who were much sought after by *nāgasvaram* artists in the early 1920s to make their instruments were Vadivelu Achari and Ranganatha Achari in a village called Narasingapuram near Mayiladuthurai. In the production course, the artisans select high-quality wood and it is first cut into blocks. The cut blocks are turned on the lathe machine. The inner part of stick is removed by piercing it with a sharp-edged file. The body part of *nāgasvaram* is made into a shape of a pipe by removing the inner wood pulp. Then the hollowed wooden stick is smoothened and cleaned with normal water. Once the long hollow-shaped body is made, seven holes are drilled on the body. In addition, five more holes are drilled at the bottom. Finally it is smoothened with sand paper and mouth tip is attached at the top and a conical bore is attached at the end. The base part of *nāgasvaram,* a large flaring bell, is made of wood by turning it on a lathe machine. Upper part is said as mouth tip and is made of reed. Both, the flaring bell and the reed tip are made separately and fixed to the body of *nāgasvaram*. Narasingampettai, a small town, 40 km away from Tanjavur, is well known for the production of *nāgasvaram*. It has many well-versed artisans in making many musical instruments.

A Divine Instrument

Nāgasvaram is known as a divine instrument because there is a belief that every part of a *nāgasvaram,* there dwells a God. The circular lower round (*kizh anaisu*) represents Sūrya or the Sun God. The bore inner hole depicts Lord Viṣṇu, the upper hole (*mel-anaisu*) denotes Śakti, the body depicts Lord Brahmā, the seven holes represent the seven holy mothers in Hindu mythology and the sound (*nāda*) emanating from the instrument is Lord Śiva Himself.

Nāgasvaram of Different Materials

Nāgasvaram originally was made of stone (soap stone) and was called *kallu nayanam* and *thollu nayanam*. Being very heavy and difficult to walk around and playing it, probably, led to the instrument being converted into wood. That the artists performed before the Emperor Rājarāja Chozha used stone *nāgasvaram*s is on record and it was suggested by some artists to change the instrument from stone to wood for the sake of convenience according to historians have also been accepted by musicologists. A *nāgasvaram* made in stone was played till the late 1960s at the Kumbheśvara Temple at Kumbakoṇam.

This stone *nāgasvaram* was played by V. Kunjithapadam Pillai. He died about thirty years ago and playing on the stone instrument has been stopped since then. It is on display at the Endowment Officer's office and it is believed that it is demonstrated for special visitors by the *nāgasvaram vidvān* Sri Swaminatha Pillai (who is attached to the temple for more than twenty years now).

The difference between the wooden *nāgasvaram* and the stone *nāgasvaram* is that the wooden *nāgasvaram* has seven finger holes while one on stone has only six. The latter can play only six *svara*s (notes). Only *pradhi madhyamam* (the note *Ma*) can be played. *Śuddha madhyamam* cannot be played, whereas in the wooden *nāgasvaram* both *pradhi madhyamam* and *śuddha madhyamam* can be played.

There were also a few *nāgasvaram*s made in ivory, gold and silver with the purpose of honouring reputed *nāgasvaram* artists by kings, patrons and landlords those days. Some artists still have them at home. One such *nāgasvaram* made of ivory and gifted by Rājarāja Chozha is with the family of T. Latchappa Pillai. It is in the safety vault of a bank and during an interview with *Sampradāya* in the year 2011 he displayed it to the audience and also played it.*

Types of Nāgasvaram

Nādasvaram are made in different sizes (*figs.* 15 and 16). *Timiri nādasvaram,* a smaller version, is made in Mayiladuthurai at a place called Therezhundur where we find the famous Viṣṇu Temple of Lord Parimelazhagar (*fig.* 17). *Thimiri* is shorter in length — about 18-20 inches in length and its pitch is 5 or "G". *Bāri,* a bigger variety, is made at Narasiṅgapuram near Mayiladuthurai. *Bāri*

* One such *nāgasvaram* is at the Thiruvarur Temple as well.

is longer than *thimri* — about 2.5 feet in length. Its pitch varies from 2 to 3, i.e. "D""D" sharp and "E". Playing on a lower pitch is less strenuous and easy, hence *bāri* is the most commonly used *nāgasvarams* nowadays. There is also a middle type, known as *idai bāri* or the medium *bāri*.

Mukha-vīṇā

Mukha-vīṇā is the oldest among the wood-wind instrument and according to musicologists *nāgasvaram* is a revised version of *mukha-vīṇā*. It is also referred as the miniature *nāgasvaram* by some musicologists. It is a smaller version of both *thimiri* and *bāri*, and a much higher pitch than both of them. Hence it needs a lot of stamina and effort to play it. Because of this hardship, there are no takers for this instrument nowadays.

Mukha-vīṇā is played in some of the very big and ancient Vaiṣṇavite temples in Tamil Nadu as a part of the Vaiṣṇava Sampradāya and is particularly played in the night while the presiding deity is all set to sleep. The Śayanotsava Pūjā and Ekandam are some of the names by which these rituals are known by.

This instrument was played in Śrī Bālagopāla Temple, Guruvayur (*fig.* 18) and Śrīpadmanābhaswāmi Temple, Trivandrum in Kerala and Śrī Kr̥ṣṇa Temple, Udupi in Karnataka (all Viṣṇu temples) some years ago, and in Tamil Nadu a *mukha-vīṇā* made out of stone is still believed to be played in the very ancient and famous Vaiṣṇava temple Āḷvārthirunagari Temple in Tirunelveli. It is also played occasionally at Vaidīsvarakoil (Śiva Temple near Chidambaram).

Mukha-vīṇā was played at the Kāñcī Kāmakoṭi Maṭha by Sri Govindaraja Pillai till the late 1970s everyday for all the religious functions till the death of the "Mahā Periāwāḷ" the then pontiff — Sri Chandra Shekara Swamigal of the Śaṅkarācārya Maṭha. This ritual has been stopped completely now.

Compared to *mukha-vīṇā, nāgasvaram,* of course, continues to be played at the *maṭha* three to four times a day — early morning 5.30, morning when the Śaṅkarācārya performs his morning rituals, evening at 5.30 and night after 7.30, approximately about half an hour for each session, and on special occasions like festivals, the performance gets longer. Sri Velu is the *nāgasvaram* artist attached to the *maṭha* for many years now. His *guru* Kodavasal Sri Govindaraja Pillai was the *mukha-vīṇā* player.

The Techniques of Nāgasvaram Playing

The system of fingering adopted in *nāgasvaram* is very similar to that of flute. In flute, the semi-tones and the quarter tones are produced by partially opening or closing the finger holes. Whereas, in *nāgasvaram* the semi-tones and quarter tones are produced skilfully adjusting to the pressure of the air that is blown out. Oboe, a wind instrument belonging to the West, corresponds to *nāgasvaram*. The semi-tones in oboe are produced by manipulating the keys.

But in *nāgasvaram* there are no such keys. It can be played only by taking rigorous practice in *akaram* and *tutukaram* (puffs of air), and *tannakaram* and *gamakam* (graced rendering of notes). The above four exercises are practised by the learners of vocal during the beginning of their training by giving a lot of importance for the free movements in the vocal chords so as to highlight the nuances of *rāga*s.

As playing the instrument has a lot to do with breath control *gamaka*s (oscillations of notes) in their vicinity and transitional stages between two notes (*janta svaram*) can be played to perfection in the instrument. Fast *svara* (notes) rolls known as *brikas*, using the *viraḷ-adi* (tapping finger) on the holes, are the feature of *nāgasvaram* playing.

Nāgasvaram players usually perform solo or as a duo with a percussion instrument known as *tavil* (drum) that provides the drone note to keep a constant pitch (*śruti*), a timekeeper (*tāla/jalarā*) for the performer. This instrument, consists of a pair of metal cymbals is mostly made in bronze. The timekeeper should always be on the alert and never to get distracted.

Śruti (called *śruti petti*) gives the pitch support to *nāgasvaram* these days. It is a little box, light in weight and is hung on the shoulders when the players are on the move. *Śruti petti* is a small version of the old harmonium without the keys. It is used to keep the pitch constant.

For a very long time almost till the late 1960s *otthu* was used for *śruti*. It looked exactly like *nāgasvaram* and the player had to go on playing (blowing) it non-stop, sometimes even for six-seven hours, which was very strenuous and tiring. It was not lucrative also. *Othu* is completely out of use now.

The Nāgasvaram Band

The *nāgasvaram* "set or band" is of two types — *peria melam* (big band) and *chinna melam* (small band). *Peria melam* is consisted of two *nādasvaram* performers usually comprising of one senior artist and another, his accompaniment, a junior artist. For the percussion side, they are accompanied by two *tavil* artists. To provide the drone note or *śruti* (pitch) an artist plays *śruti petti*. As we have seen already, till the late 1960s, for the pitch, *otthu* was played as the drone note (to maintain constant pitch). To keep up time or *laya* (beats), the timekeeper played the cymbals (*jalarā*). Sometimes, if it was a big function or if the function required a *kidi-kiṭṭi* (pair of conical drums) and sometimes a conch player also became a part of the big band.

Chinna melam is comprised of one *nāgasvaram*, one *tavil*, drone note and a timekeeper. The small band is commonly played in the routine or regular temple rituals or small functions like a *gr̥ha-praveśa* (house warming) and birthdays.

There was also another set known as *nayandi melam* that was performed during temple festivals to provide music support for dance dramas, street plays, etc. (mostly folk music). In the villages, during the festivals of Māriamman (local presiding goddess), the percussive instruments like *udukai, pampai tharai* and *thappattai* with *nāgasvaram* as the main instrument were played sometimes. These festivals were generally observed on new-moon or full-moon days to ward off the evil.

These instruments were used to create loud sound and more to cause fear and frenzy among the devotees who would go into a trance often with the many percussive instruments. This tradition or ritual is still practised in the Kālī temples of Tamil Nadu villages, especially during festivals in the months of Adi (between 15 July and 15 August) and Thai (between 15 January and 15 February).

During the main temple festivals, also called *utsavams*, particularly in very big and old temples like Tanjavur, Thiruvarur, Thiruvannamalai, Kāñcīpuram and Tirupati, on the inaugural or concluding day, ten or more sets of *nāgasvaram* artists (*peria melam*) perform, leading the procession in which the deity is brought out of the temple. All the artists join together in *rakti* and *mallāri*, after which one by one, each set performs according to their seniority for a given time. This arrangement enables the artists to take the much needed break, because walking, performing and carrying the instrument — especially when the procession may take ten to twelve hours to get back to the temple — can be quite stressful.

Nāgasvaram: How It Is Taught

Learning of *nāgasvaram* starts on the Vijayadaśamī day, which is traditionally the day of *vidyārambha*. The new students desirous of learning come over to the *guru*'s place and after taking blessings from the *guru*, they begin their first class. The class may last only for a short time but being an auspicious day they have to commence that day and it is mandatory to attend the next day at least for a few minutes as a formality (and continuity).

Vocal music is mandatory for an artist aspiring to learn *nāgasvaram*. A student must learn vocal for at least three years. The idea is that he understands the *sāhitya bhāva* (meaning of the lyrics). The emphasis on vocal is to make sure that the students learn *rāgas* (songs) to emulate singing. A beginner in *nāgasvaram* starts by playing the cymbals first and thus is taught all the basics in *tāla*. Normally, learning the techniques of *tāla* takes a long time. Once a student is thorough with the basics of *tāla*, he starts his *abhyāsa* (learning) in *nāgasvaram*.

(To hold breath for a long time in olden days, a very interesting exercise was taught. A student was given a long lotus stem and was asked to blow it for a long time holding his breath as much as he could. This used to go on for several hours a day till the student was ready for the next. The timekeeping and vocal were the next exercises.)

After these rigorous exercises, when a student is

---

* Compiled from several interviews with some of the *nāgasvaram* artists.

familiar with *abhyāsa-gānam* (beginner's music), he starts with the *nāgasvaram* instrument (*figs.* 19-20). After coming to a senior level the teacher would get another student or performer as *edhir nayanam* to play together exchange of *svaras* and other nuances of the instrument so as to get ready for performances.

The Nāgasvaram Worship*

To most of the *nāgasvaram* artists their art is their God. One artist in an interview said: *seyyum thozhile devam* (our profession is our God). Many of these artists believe in performing a little *pūjā* (ritual) before they begin their daily practice. As we have seen earlier, the artists believe that in every part of *nāgasvaram*, there resides a God and hence the instrument is an object worthy of worship.

Vermilion or sandal paste or turmeric is applied on the holes; but even for that some rules are observed. Vermilion is applied on the first hole, second, then three spots at the *keezhanusu*. Overall the belief is that the turmeric and vermilion should be placed in odd numbers like one or five, but never in eight, and three though it is an odd number. The application of turmeric is a synonym of applying it on the forehead (*śiras*) and feet of God. They light *agarbattīs* (waive the smoke of incense) in the room where the instrument is kept and offer some flowers as they do to the deity they worship and then with a pure mind pick up the instrument in their hands and start to play.

On all the nine days of the Navarātri they spend more time in *pūjā* as they perform for goddesses Sarasvatī, Lakṣmī and Durgā. On the ninth day the instrument is cleaned well and decorated with flowers, etc. and made to rest along with books related to music. On the tenth day, the day of Vijayadaśamī, *prasādas* like sweets and fruits are offered to Goddess Sarasvatī as well as the instrument along with the music books.

On the Vijayadaśamī day the artistes also perform at their house, in class or school, for some time, in a concert pattern and conclude with *madyamavatī rāgam*. A number of Dhikshitar *kr̥tis* dedicated to "Ambal" is played. They play to the accompaniment of *tavil*. This exclusive concert is their offering to Goddess Sarasvatī as a Navarātri Pūjā ritual.

Maintenance of Nāgasvaram

Nāgasvaram calls for daily care and thus is cleaned everyday with a soft mull or a silk piece of "pure" cloth (they use the word "pure" keeping in mind the sanctity of the instrument). Now and then a little water is applied and with a piece of soft cloth, it is also cleaned internally too. The artists then apply some pure sesame oil (no other oil is allowed) at the entrance of the openings (holes) and using a soft cloth piece, they clean the holes as well. Care is taken to ensure that oil does not go inside the pipe during the process, but is applied only at the entrance of the holes. Externally, oil is rubbed all over and it is more or less like a massage to preserve the wood and also to get *nāgasvaram* a good sheen.

The instruments have specially-made covers, according to their sizes. After the performance, the artist makes it sure that the instrument is put back in its cover and is neatly tied up. A lot of care is taken in ensuring the quality of the cloth by which the cover is made, as the artists do a lot of travelling with their instruments. Care is also taken to make sure that the instrument is protected from insects like termites. In short, the instrument is treated as something very precious and sacred by the artists.

2

Accompanying Instruments

AMONG the many art forms in Carnatic music there are many instruments that are played as accompanying instruments. These accompanying instruments are known as *pāka vādyam* and considered as the main accompanying instruments. During the earlier days for vocal the main accompaniments were *vīṇā* or flute and *mṛdaṅgam*. Much later violin substituted *vīṇā* and flute. Then *upa-vādyams* (additional accompaniments) were introduced. This was introduced particularly for percussion like *kañjira*, *gatam*, morsing, *ḍholaka* and sometimes even *tablā*. For vocal, we have the percussive *upa-vādyams* only. But for dance, *upa-vādyams* like flute, harmonium and *vīṇā* are used.

Nāgasvaram, from the beginning, had only *tavil* as an accompaniment. Even though many artistes have experimented with *mṛdaṅgam*, *ḍholaka*, etc. these instruments have not been able to fill in or fit into the place of *tavil*. In earlier times, an instrument called *kiḍi kaṭṭi* was also played along with *tavil*. Now it is no more in use. Depending upon the situations, few more accompanying instruments are used in a *nāgasvaram* concert in temple festivals now. Among them are *daṅgi*, *eḍakka*, *jalarā*, *kanaka thappattai*, *kudi-melam*, *muttu*, *pañca-mukha vādyam*, *śaṅkhu* and *śuddha maddalam*.

Tavil

Tavil is also known as the "mother of all *laya* instruments" (*fig.* 21). It makes *tavil* a perfect match to the magnificence of *nāgasvaram* in its sound, effect and divinity. No replacement has worked out for *tavil* so far, or no other musical instrument has satisfied the music lovers to play with *nāgasvaram*.

Nāgasvaram and *tavil* are made for each other and are inseparable and compliment each other in every way. Hence in a book dedicated to *nāgasvaram*, it is only appropriate to give some details about *tavil*.

Tavil is a percussive instrument made out of jackfruit wood and animal skin, and is used as a rythmic accompaniment to *nāgasvaram*. It is a must for *nāgasvaram* and no *nāgasvaram* can be imagined or played without *tavil*.

A very unique feature of *tavil* is that while other percussive instruments accompany the main instrument, *tavil* artist begins to play first and then the main artist — *nāgasvaram* player — takes cue and begins to play. The *tavil* artist begins playing *tāla* (beats) in which the *nāgasvaram* artist is about to present his piece. So there should be a lot of understanding between them, and there should be a total synchronization between the two instruments.

To play *tavil*, one needs sound technical knowledge about the nuances of *laya*. There are a lot of mathematical calculations involved in playing this instrument. An important fact to be noted is that this instrument has set guidelines for all other percussion instruments. Hence *tavil* is popularly called as "the mother of all percussion instruments".

Today, even though *nāgasvaram* has taken a back seat, *tavil* to a certain extent has remained active because the instrument, that was hitherto only an accompaniment to *nāgasvaram*, is how used by other instrument players like mandolin, saxophone, violin and sometimes even by the

Bharatanāṭyam dancers in their concerts. This kind of fusion has become popular these days.

The Role of Tavil (with Nāgasvaram) in Temple Rituals

When the deity of the temple is brought out from the *sanctum sanctorum,* the practice in any temple is for the *tavil* artist to play *aḷarippu* first. It is just a series of *jāti*s (beats said orally in dance) in a systematic pattern. This *aḷarippu* differs from the *aḷarippu* that is performed by the Bharatanāṭyam artists on the stage.

Aḷarippu was known as *mellaprapatti* in olden days and this was the first item to be performed in a dance recital. Likewise, *aḷarippu* had to be performed by the *tavil* artists in their recitals. This item will always be set in the five *attcharas* (beats) and set in *kandagati* (*tāla* pattern). The significance of the five beats is that they make the devotee aware that God is Supreme to the five forms — earth, water, air, fire and ether, and all important features attached to these forms.

Any temple ritual should begin in this number form and has been prescribed by the Āgamas with due explanations. This five-number system is followed in both the Vaiṣṇavite and Śaivite temples. These details are all given by several *tavil* artists. As such there is no independent role for *tavil*. It is only a "puckā Vādyam" — accompanying instrument.

Kiḍi Kaṭṭi

This is an age-old instrument and is almost unheard of in the Tamil Nadu temples nowadays. This was very much in usage as an accompaniment to *nāgasvaram* and played along with *tavil* till about forty years ago. It played an important role in *peria melam* especially when the *tavil* artist had to do the *laya-vinyāsa* (highlights of that particular *tāla*).

thānī āvarttana (played exclusively by percussive artists to give the main vocalist or artist a break and also showcase their expertise) on *kiḍi-kiṭṭi* was highly appreciated by music lovers.

Kiḍi kaṭṭi is consisted of a pair of conical drums and looks very much like *tavil*. It is played with two bent sticks, instead of hands. Even in those days very few people had mastered on this instrument which was very popular with the temple worship. This is the same mentioned in *Tevaram* as *koḍukaṭṭi* which means, that which is struck with a stick. This instrument is occasionally used in the Thiruvarur Temple. One temple where this instrument is still heard is at the Kilvelur Kedily Appar Temple where it is a part of the daily music ritual. But it is done more as a part of the daily ritual, just taken out by somebody (not a trained artist) from the *nāgasvaram* group. He just beats the instrument a few times and put it back in its cover. This instrument has not been played since 1975 and the last artist who played this instrument was Shri Naṭeśa Pillai.

Nāgasvaram Accompaniments during Temple Rituals

DAṄGI

It is played as a percussion accompaniment to *nāgasvaram* and *mukha-vīṇā*, smaller version of *nāgasvaram*. This instrument was used to play at Udupi Śrīkr̥ṣṇa Temple (Karnataka) till recently.

EḌAKKA

This instrument (*fig.* 22) is used as an accompaniment to *nāgasvaram* only in a few temples like Guruvayur Śrī Bālagopāla Temple in Kerala.

JALARĀ

This instrument belongs to the family of cymbals and is

made up of two metal plates. This is used for keeping up the tempo beats (time- or *tāla*-keeper) and is commonly used for *nāgasvaram, bhajana,* group singing, etc.

KANAKA THAPPATTAI

It is a percussion instrument belonging to the *kañjira* family. This is a single-faced open drum to which skin is stitched over a circular ring of thin strips of bamboo. It is played during Lord Tyāgarāja's dance procession at Thiruvarur. It was also a very popular instrument in the Śiva temples of Sri Lanka and was used as an accompaniment (*upa-vādyam*) to *nāgasvaram* and *tavil* many years ago.

KUDI-MELAM

This percussion instrument is also known as *koil melam* (temple *melam*) and is often used in the temple festivals as a part of the *nāgasvaram* band.

MUTTU

This is a smaller version of *mr̥daṅgam* and was regularly featured in the Thiruvarur Temple during temple festivals. This percussion instrument accompanied *nāgasvaram* when the presiding deity Lord Tyāgeśa was taken out in the palanquin. It was also played at the Thiruvaniyur (Chennai) for the presiding deity, again Lord Tyāgeśa, and the beats were known as *ādum* (dancing) Tyāgeśa and *odum* (running) Tyāgeśa.

PAÑCAMUKHA VĀDYAM

This massive percussion instrument is found only in two temples —.one at Thiruvarur and the other at Thiruthuraipoondi near Thiruvarur. During the days of Ramaswami Dikshitar it was an accompaniment for *nāgasvaram* and the rituals to play was formatted by Ramaswami Dikshitar and later his son Muthuswamy

Dikshitar. It is only on display and is just played on certain festivals as a ritual (*fig.* 23).

ŚAṄKHU

It is the conch and is used as the *upa-pakkā-vādyam* (additional or optional) for *nāgasvaram* (*fig.* 24) and is still played in some temples as a part of the ritual.

ŚUDDHA MADDALAM

Śuddha maddalam accompanied *nāgasvaram* on very special occasions at Thiruvarur. Today, it is just done as a formality for a few minutes on certain festivals.

Orchestra

One of the best events to have taken place in the history of Indian classical music is the development of "orchestra" — several instruments coming together and performing together. The possibilities for this evolution could have happened due to two important factors. One, there was no mike system those days. So, with many instruments the concerts had a better effect on the audience. Two, the idea of having a standard and definite proportion of the number of wind instruments, percussion instruments, stringed instruments together must have brought in the desired, pleasing and melodious effect, and also making it more audible in places like temples, wedding halls and in open air.

During the Bhakti movement group singing also became very popular and had a better effect on the devotees. One lead singer would sing and others would follow him/her. This system came to be called as *bhajana sampradāya,* popularizing group singing.

This group singing brought together like-minded devotees in the neighbourhood. They would walk towards the temple singing hymns together early in the mornings during the month of Marghazi (December–January). Slowly they included instruments like *śruti, tāla,* harmonium, *ḍholaka* (percussion) and so on. Some of the composers also created special compositions that could be sung in group for a better effect.

Indian music is essentially melodic in character and "orchestral music" is the absolute music in its purest form. Take for example one of Saint Tyāgarāja's most popular *gāna-rāga pañcaratna-kṛtis* — in Ārabhi Rāga — *sadiñcane o mānasa*. The effect of this classical piece when rendered by a vocalist, an instrumentalist and finally by an orchestra — any music lover will feel the enriched effect of the group singing with full orchestra far more interesting.

This song along with the other four compositions is performed on the occasion of the birth anniversary celebrations of the saint in January every year. Hundreds of musicians and devotees visit Thiruvaiyaru to participate in the celebration and perform together. Those, who have witnessed the Tyāgarāja *ārādhanā** performed at Thiruvaiyaru (*fig.* 25) and have heard the rendering of the above-mentioned song, would agree of the electrifying effect they have experienced. Hundreds of singers, violinists, *mṛdaṅga* players, *nāgasvaram* artists, *vīṇā* artists, flautists, *tavil* players, *gatam* players, etc. join together.

The whole effect is mesmerizing, magical and magnificent because you have the most popular artists, without any discrimination, among music lovers, students, young performers, singing in unison and paying their tribute to the saint on the banks of the Kāverī River, which has been a quiet witness to this divine music ritual for several decades.

---

* This Tyāgarāja *ārādhanā* held around the second and third week of January every year is telecast live in the Doordarshan network and watched by millions of music lovers all over the world.

On account of quality, effect and strength, orchestra always has more appeal especially for the mass. The other advantage is that compositions can be made popular when performed in an orchestra. Besides, it gives an opportunity for the main artist to accommodate more instruments (*upa-tāla vādya*) in the orchestra. The audience also gets to know and learn more about the tone, colour, techniques and details of other instruments. There is also a healthy competition among the artists to come out with their best performance, giving the listeners a rare, delightful and divine experience.

In olden days eighteen (*aṣṭa-daśa*) instruments were played in the temples during the Āgamas (rituals) in some temples. In the Brahadambal Temple at Pudukoṭṭai thirty-two instruments were played during festivals. The sound of this orchestra would be carried over even to neighbouring villages those days so they could also join in. In fact, it was a way of giving signal that the *pūjā* had started.

Orchestra and Nāgasvaram

Orchestras, in big forms and small forms, have been in existence in India from very early times. We read about *bṛnda gānam* and *vaṁśaka bṛndam* in the early literatures. There have made mentions of dance-dramas, dance performances in ancient literatures where vocalists have performed with a lot of instruments. Even in the courts of kings, dancers have performed to the accompaniment of big or small orchestra comprising of several instruments (varieties).

In north India, *naubhāṭ* (comprising of nine performers) performed in palaces, mansions, mosques and even near the arched gateway of cities during the Mughal period. Mughal history has placed on record that Emperor Akbar used to derive great pleasure from *naubhāṭ* performances.

We can compare this to *chinna melam* and *peria melam* which started some years later and also acquired the name — the Tanjavur Band (probably the influence of the British Band) that was played and practised at Fort St. George in Madras in the early seventeenth century.

This band inspired Muthuswamy Dikshitar to compose more than thirty-five notes in Śaṅkarābharaṇam in the Western style which is still played by the *nāgasvaram* sets in temple festivals and wedding processions. In fact, there is a small *notusvara* song *santatam pahimam saṅgīta śyāmale* attuned exactly like the British National Anthem — "God save the Queen". These *notusvara*s are taught to the young children in the beginning stage of learning music, both vocal and instrument (*abhyāsa-gānam*).

It is also noteworthy to mention that Muthuswamy Dikshitar introduced the Western violin in Carnatic music as an accompaniment. His younger brother Baleswamy Dikshitar learnt to play the violin and became proficient in it. The *nāgasvaram* rituals, in playing *nāgasvaram,* that were formatted by Dikshitar at the Thiruvarur Temple, are being followed to this day. In all the orchestras mentioned above, the instruments merely repeated the chosen tune and occasionally doubled them in the octaves. The number of performers would range from five to fifteen.

As we have already seen, *tavil* was the principal accompanying instrument to *nāgasvaram.* There are many other percussive instruments that accompany *nāgasvaram.* They perform mostly during the temple festivals especially when the deity is brought out to the streets and taken around in a procession. Some accompaniments are still in use while some are not, owing to the fact that for these arts there are no takers.

3

Temple Festivals and Nāgasvaram Traditions

THERE are three aspects to every festival in our country. The first is the ritualistic aspect that belongs to the various steps of its celebration, whether it is at home or in temple — the preliminary arrangements, the performance of *pūjā,* etc.

The second is the legendary aspect, i.e. the ancient stories that had grown around it: the origin and reasons for celebrating the festival in society and temples, and at homes. For example, this aspect reminds us of the significance of festivals like Divālī (return of Śrī Rāma after his *vana-vāsa* and his victory over Rāvaṇa), Janmāṣṭamī (birthday of Lord Kṛṣṇa), Navarātri (nine-day celebrations and worship of Goddess Durgā), Vināyaka Caturthī (birthday of Lord Gaṇeśa) and so on.

The third is the philosophical or the esoteric aspect that gives full significance to the celebration and has kept it live through many centuries and generations.

The people of Tamil Nadu have a way of remembering and honouring great personalities — by observing their birth or death anniversaries. The Vaiṣṇavites celebrate the birth anniversaries of the Āḷvārs and *ācārya*s, while the Śaivites celebrate or observe the death anniversaries of the sixty-three Nāyanmārs and *ācārya*s.

There are monthly festivals attached to one important star (*nakṣatra*) every month like Thai Pūsam (January–February),

Māsi Magam (February–March), Panguni Utaram (March–April) and so on. There are also festivals that usher in seasons like the spring (March–April) (Vasantotsava), harvest season (Poṅgal), nine days of Navarātri, monsoon Aipasimasam (November) and so on.

Besides these, we have festivals to offer special rituals to the rivers during a particular month on the full-moon day or on the new-moon day like the Kumbha Melā when millions of devotees take a dip in rivers like the Gaṅgā (at the Triveṇī Saṅgam in Allahabad — the confluence of three rivers, the Gaṅgā, Yamunā and the mystical Sarasvatī River). In Tamil Nadu, November is full of festivals associated with the Kāverī River, called Kada Muzhaku and Muda Muzhaku, and on the eighteenth day of Ādi month (July–August).

Festivals seem to constitute the eternal spirit of India. We do not know when exactly festivals came into existence but we can say that festivals must have started right from the time human beings organized themselves into a civilized group or community or a society.

Festivals are the outward social expressions of communal joy and have retained the best of past culture, art and traditions, and have handed it over to generations to come. There is continuity in festival celebrations and several factors have contributed to these festivals, because most of the festivals are connected to religion and temples. Festivals, mostly conservative, do not lend themselves easily to changes but continue to be rigid and an open window to the past. All the temple festivals involve the entire society around, through daily religious rituals like *ārādhanā* and music rituals such playing *nāgasvaram*, singing devotional hymns, taking part in the processions in and outside the temple, visiting relatives and ancestral homes, and reviving ties with relatives and so on.

These are not mere celebrations but involve devotees in social and cultural activities. These festivals have been going on for centuries even long before the spirit of nationhood. With times there have been a number of changes in the festivities but the mode of observance of festivals remains the same.

In the cultural observance we have music, instruments, discourses, dance, dramas, street plays and colourful pageants in the form of the local temple deity's visit outside the temple into the town.

In the religious observance, the quintessential components are oil lamps, delicious offerings (*prasāda*), incense, camphor, flowers, garlands, fruits, coconuts, betel leaf, turmeric, holy ash, vermilion (*kumkum*), *kolams* (*raṅgolī*) and floral decorations. The various music rituals have made their contribution in continuing and preserving the ancient culture and rich art forms.

The kings and patrons had made liberal endowments to promote all art forms. And these art forms were mainly performed in connection with the temple festivals. This did help to develop an aesthetic and literary taste among the masses (devotees) in the past. All these art forms were available free in temples like fresh air and water. These freebies not only made the devotee a peaceful and blissful soul but also brought within the human being an aesthetic sense of appreciation for all fine arts. This in a way provided continuity for the festival celebrations and the festival culture in India. Another factor for the keen interest in festivals even today is that there are a large number of temples in India and their festivals involve the entire society around them not only with religious values, but with some social values as well.

Nāgasvaram Traditions

Instrumental music has always been very popular in

temples and there have been some indigenous evidences that many instruments were played in temples from time immemorial. This music not only served to provide melody but also had a very divine effect among the devotees. The Śaiva savants (Nāyanmārs) — Appārs, Sundarārs and Sambandārs — have given a list of some of the important instruments that were played in the temples as rituals.

This kind of music and dance accompanied by various instruments like wind instruments, string instruments and percussion instruments moved the feelings and emotions of the devotees. These also aroused a sense of duty and love for preserving these art forms from extinction. There are many conventions and traditions related to the playing of *nāgasvaram* during various occasions in the temple. It should be borne in mind that only conventions and traditions have helped to preserve our rich culture throughout the centuries. Conventions and traditions have a lot of significance, values and meaning. And these conventions have enabled us to live a peaceful, harmonious and meaningful life.

Nāgasvaram is an inevitable musical instrument in almost all temple rituals. Beginning from early morning to the closing of the temple at late night, *nāgasvaram* gets played for every ritual. There is an unwritten rule specifying the music for the hour of the day and that particular day. This has been in force for many centuries so much so that when people listen to the music far away from the temple, they at once know what kind of *pūjā* (ritual) is taking place in the temple. *Nāgasvaram* is a very loud instrument and its sound travels a long distance. So, even though one may not be listening particularly to that music, it falls on his ears and reminds him of the ritual or the worship.

The *nāgasvaram* rituals in the Vaiṣṇavite and Śaivite temples are similar except in:

In Vaiṣṇava temples, *heccarika* is played; but in Śaiva temples, it is not. In Vaiṣṇava temples Vasanta Rāga is played during the *dīpārādhanā.*

In Śaiva temples *Thirupugazh* or *Tevaram* hymn is mandatory after Mallāri while in Vaiṣṇava temples *heccarika* is compulsory especially if the festival continues to the next day.

The music at daybreak is *tirupallieluci* (waking up the Lord) in Bhūpāla Rāga in all the temples. The very structure of this *rāga* is most thrilling. The *rāga* is formed to represent the lotus flower that gently opens its petals to welcome the rays of the slowly ascending morning sun. It is a great wonder as to how this *rāga* was conceived in this manner and so shaped. Only those who have enjoyed the Bhūpāla Rāga, can imagine the beauty of the opening of the lotus petals.

Bhūpāla is *Purnirmai-pann* of *Tevaram* (Tamil hymn) and, going a few centuries earlier in time, it was known as the *pann-notiram* in the Saṅgam anthology "Paripadal". Thus Bhūpāla has taken a long way travelling under different names from the second century to the twentieth century indicating the astonishing fact as to how the culture of the Tamil people has been harmoniously continuing for such a long period.

After the wake up song, the *nāgasvaram* artist plays *rāga*s like Revaguptī and Bowli. Following the wake up ritual is the *ārādhanā* (bathing, dressing of the Lord) for which *rāga*s like Bilahārī, Dhanyāsi and Malayamarutam are played. At midday *ārādhanā* (*ucci-kāla pūjā*), the time when the Lord goes for a siesta or rest, soothing tunes like Madhyamavatī and Surutti (*sendurutti-pann*) are played, after which the temple is closed till about 4 p.m.

During the evening *pūjā* (*sāyaratcai pūjā*) Pūrvīkalyāṇī,

Kedāragaula and Śaṅkarābharaṇam are played. In some temples the deity is taken along the inner corridors of the temple every evening with the *nāgasvaram* artist performing, accompanied by *tavil*. The usual procedure is that the deity will go around thrice and then stop just outside the *sanctum sanctorum* for some time while the music will go on for about half an hour at least.

Another important music pattern followed by *nāgasvaram* and *tavil* is as follows: when the deity (*utsava-mūrti*) is brought out from the *sanctum sanctorum, mallāri* is played. When we say that the deity is brought out, it should be remembered that in every temple there are two deities. The main deity — known as the *mūlāvar* stone idol — permanently placed in the *sanctum sanctorum*. The *utsava-mūrti* — a replica of the main presiding deity — is made in bronze for the purpose of taking it out for procession during the festival days.

The *mallāri* is first played before lifting the deity and then the deity is placed on a *mañjam* (a couch). Lifting and carrying the deity with the couch can be very taxing as the bronze idol and the metal couch are very heavy. It needs a minimum of four to eight people to lift it on their shoulders with the help of long heavy wooden or bamboo poles.

MALLĀRI

The *mallāri* music of *nāgasvaram*, usually is played in the Nattai Rāga, has its unique structure and significance. The *mallāri* is a majestic musical form played to mark the different stages of worship in temples as such. It is a musical form without any *sāhitya* (lyrics or words in the composition).

Mallāri is necessarily played in temples to indicate the commencement of a particular worship or commencement of a particular ritual. When the commencement of the deity's procession begins, it is called *purappadu* (getting ready to leave). It can either be within the four walls of the temple or outside, around the four streets wherein the temple lies centred.

Mallāri comprises of three or four speeds — slow, medium, fast and sometimes a variation with a different gait like the majestic walk of an emperor when he walks surveying his subjects in an enjoyable beat.

There are several *mallāri* is played for different rituals like:

- *sādhāraṇa mallāri* (regular or common)
- *tīrtha mallāri* (when holy water is served)
- *taer mallāri* (when the temple car is taken). All the three are common with both the Śaiva and Vaiṣṇava temples.
- *thaligai mallāri* (This is performed only in the Vaiṣṇava temples and happens when *naivedya* (food) is offered to God.)
- *kumbha mallāri* (This was very popular in both Śaiva and Vaiṣṇava temples, particularly during the days of the *devadāsīs*. They used to hold the *pūrṇa-kumbha* silver pot with fresh mango leaves in their hands and danced while the deity was taken around.)
- *Tiruputta tāla mallāri* (This is based on seven beats and is normally played when the procession is about to start. The beats can be "*takita-thaka-dhimi*" (3 + 4) or "*thaka-dhimi-thakita*" (4 + 3).)

All other *mallāri*s do not have any specific structure or pattern (beats). It all depends on the performers' creativity and imagination.

In south Indian music system and tradition we do not find this particular *nādasvaram* tradition in any other instruments or vocal music.

At one time, almost a century ago, when Carnatic music

concerts were not formatted systematically, the highlight of *nāgasvaram* was the *rakti melam* and the artists played for hours and even days together elaborating the nuances of the *rāgas*. Such is the greatness of *nāgasvara*!

The *devadāsī* system was abolished about sixty years ago, hence there is no dance but *nādasvaram* with the *mallāri* rituals still continue and enthrall the devotees and music lovers, and the priests carry *pūrṇa-kumbha*. The *pūrṇa-kumbha* ritual is performed not only in temples and *maṭhas* but also on occasions like receiving some dignitaries, diplomats during cultural and social festivities as a mark of respect. *Pūrṇa-kumbha* is always accompanied by *nāgasvaram* and when not possible the recorded music of *nāgasvaram* is at least played.

The *rāga* played during *mallāri* is Gambhīra Nattai. But *tālas* can be different like *ganta, tripuṭa* and so on. *Mallāri* is played in three speeds and is like *aḷarippu* that is the invocatory item in a dance concert, more as a warming up exercise of the artist.

Tālas prescribed to be played for these are *tripuṭa, miśra, kanda* and *ādi tāla*. *Mallāri* cannot be played in any other *rāga* other than Gambhīra Nattai. It is set to this tune because as the name of the *rāga* itself suggests (*gambhīra*, meaning majestic) because of its overtones of force and heroism.

From the moment of lifting the deity on the shoulders, Nattai Rāga, Ārabhi Rāga, Śrī Rāga and Varali Rāga are played. On special days like Friday, new moon, full moon or birthdays of the Āḷvārs or Nāyanmārs the deity will also be taken out.

Another important factor is that no procession, whether a regular ritual or a temple pageant involving big processions can begin without playing *mallāri*. This explains its presence and priority in *peria melam*. A very interesting fact is that when the *nāgasvaram* artist, accompanied by *tavil*, plays *mallāri*, the total effect of the music is such that it inspires the carriers of the deity. Now they feel the heaviness of the deity is totally lost, and with an unusual heroic spirit the men who lift and carry the deity do it at great ease.

Here is one such ritual that will prove the effect of *mallāri.* At Nachiarkoil near Mayiladuthurai, the presiding deity is Lord Viṣṇu and the Garuḍa finds a very special and unique place in this temple. (The temple is one among the 108 Tirupatis and has been personified by the Āḷvārs in their *Nāḷāyira Divya Prabandham.*) This temple is unique for two reasons. One, as the *utsava-mūrti* and the *mūlava mūrti* of Garuḍa are the same and are made in stone. Normally, the *utsava-mūrti* is a smaller version of *mūlava mūrti* and is made of *pañcalauha* (five metals). The Garuḍa is a beautifully carved idol in granite and is massive and heavy in size. Once a year for a particular festival, the Kal Garuḍan (stone-Garuḍa), as he is known, is brought out from his *sanctum sanctorum* and as he ascends the first step only four people carry him. In the second step eight people have to carry, in the third step it becomes sixteen and in the final step it becomes sixty-four and you find that even the sixty-four are unable to carry it due to its heaviness and they struggle to lift the deity. Again when the deity gets back into the *sanctum sanctorum,* the number dwindles from sixty-four to four when it reaches the final step. For those who have witnessed this event, it is a "believe it or not" experience. *Nāgasvaram* is played during the whole process with the beats. The entire ritual is beyond comprehension and is mentioned here to show the effect of music on the carriers of the Garuḍa.

There is a scheduled pattern of stopping on each street beginning from the east and on each side of the street corner. This schedule of systematic, organized way of playing particular *rāga*s makes people around aware, merely by listening to *rāga*, of the position as to where the deity has reached in course of the procession.

Finally, when the deity goes to the *palli-arai* (bed-chamber), Nilāmbarī Rāga is played. This is the Megha Rāga *kuriñji pann* and the song is called *kadavai-paṭṭu* song for closing up. This ritual is known as the Śayanotsava or *ekānta-sevā* in Vaiṣṇava temples. This *nāgasvaram* tradition that has been passed on for many generations is followed in most of the big temples even today.

Tiruvarur Temple observes the *āru-kāla-pujaigaḷ* (six *pūjās* a day) — early morning one (*uṣā kāla*) 5-6 a.m.; forenoon (*kāla sandhi*) 6-8 a.m.; noon (*ucci kāla*) 10 a.m. to 12 noon; evening (*sāya rakṣai*) 4.30-6.30 p.m.; night (*eraṇḍam kāla*) 6.30-8 p.m. and late night or midnight (*ardha-jamam*) 8.30 p.m. onwards till the closure of temple.

Totally in a day the *nāgasvaram* players play for more than six hours for the deity as a ritual on normal days. The six *pūjās* also have prescribed *rāgas* to be played:

- *Uṣā kāla* — Bhūpāla, followed by Bauli, Mayamalavagoula, Malayamarutam
- *Kāla sandhi* — Bilahāri, Kedāra, Navroz, Kuriñji Dhanyasi, Saveri, etc.
- *Ucchi kāla* — Madhyamavatī, Maniraṅgu, Śuddhabaṅgalā, etc.
- *Sāya rakṣai* — Kalyāṇī, Toḍī, Śaṅkarābharaṇam, Bhairavī, Kambhojī, etc.
- *Eraṇḍam kāla* — Ahirī, Kaṇāda, Ānanda Bhairavī, Mohana, etc.
- *Ardha-jamam* — Nīlāmbharī, Lalitā, Vasanta, etc.

Ramaswami Dikshitar, father of the great composer Muthuswamy Dikshitar, had formatted *rāgas* for the *nāgasvaram* players, *tālas* for the temple dancers (now extinct) and the percussion players of *pañca-mukha vādyam* and *śuddha maddalam*. These traditions are not strictly followed and have been cut down for the convenience of the artist and the temple authorities.

RAKTI

Rakti was a special piece played exclusively in temples by the *nāgasvaram* and *tavil* artists. *Rakti rāgas* have high melodic content. There is a special niche for playing it in *nāgasvaram* and such playing is also classified as *rakti melam*.

Rakti is a musical format without any *sāhitya* (lyrics). It is based on *tatta kāram* (rhythmic syllables) and the recommended *rāga* to be played is Nattakuriñjī. The recommended *tāla* is *miśracapu*. *Rakti* also follows the *mallāri* pattern and gives more scope to *tavil* artists to showcase their *laya* expertise. It is suited to *nāgasvaram–tavil* artists because these are played in open air mostly in temples and wedding *maṇḍapams* (huge halls). It always concludes with the *nāgasvaram* artist presenting *svaras* in *rāgamālikā* (variety of *rāgas*).

The *rakti melam* rituals were something exclusive to the Thiruvarur Temple. *Rakti* is played during all days of festivals. Once the deity is brought out of the *sanctum sanctorum* to the streets, specific *rāgas* are played, followed by *rakti melam*. *Rakti* is highlighted, particularly on the day of *ṛṣabha vāhana* (the bull carrier). Four *nāgasvarams*, accompanied by two *tavils*, play to the beat in *capu tāla*.

In Thirukadaiyur, *rakti* is different; *rāgas* and *tāla* followed are *kanda*. In the Tiruvalundur Parimalarangan Temple and Chidambaram Śrī Govindarāja Temple, both of which are Vaiṣṇavite temples, a number of *nāgasvaram* traditions are still followed. In both theses temples the Navarātri festival is observed in a grand manner. On all the nine days, the Goddess (presiding deity's consort) comes out of the *sanctum sanctorum* in all Her finery to the *maṇḍapam*.

From there she is taken around the temple to the music played by the *nāgasvaram* players. She is taken to the Perumāḷ *sannidhi* (God's *sanctum sanctorum*) when *mallāri,* followed by *rakti* and *pallavī,* is played. There the God and Goddess exchange garlands. The *arcaka* (temple priest) carries the garland on his head, dancing to the beats of *nāgasvaram* and percussion instruments which play specially composed songs for the *malaimarru* (exchange of garlands) ritual.

The specified *rāga*s for these songs are mostly Mañjī, Kuriñjī and Navroz. Everyday, five different songs are played and the ritual takes place on all nine days. When the Goddess returns to her *sanctum sanctorum,* the *thiruvandikappu* ritual is done. *Ecarika* (a particular beat in the music) is played after which the Goddess goes back into her chamber. The *lai* (lullaby) or the *uñjala* (swing) songs are played after which the temple closes. If the festival has not concluded, *mallāri* is played as an indication for the devotees.

Another popular festival where one hears a lot of *nāgasvaram* is the Ṭeppotsava (float festival). This festival is observed in a very grand manner in temples — Thiruvarur, Madurai, Thiruvidamarudur, Kumbakoṇam and Mylapore (Chennai) — that have very large tanks. One of the main traditions followed in these temples is the *nāgasvaram* orchestra going strictly by tradition of playing tunes formatted exclusively for the festival. *Nāgasvaram* is played followed by *oḍuvar*s singing the hymns. Besides this there are other cultural events such as music concerts, discourse, dance and sometimes even folk dances like the dummy horse and *karagam*. During these festivals sometimes more than ten sets of *nāgasvaram* can be seen played in the procession. *Mallāri* is played by all in unison, later each group plays for a given time according to their seniority. The Mayavaram Tulā festival is also well known (*fig*. 26).

The Brahmotsava is yet another big festival celebrated for ten-days, once a year in both Śaiva and Vaiṣṇava temples. On all the days of the festival, the main deity is taken in a procession around the main streets known as *mada-vīdhi* (streets along which the temple car is drawn). Each day, the deity is drawn on a different *vāhana* always to the music of *nāgasvaram* accompanied by the percussion instruments and sometimes singing of the sacred hymns of the Āḷvārs or the Nāyanmārs.

The famous Kapālīśvara Temple in Chennai to this day witnesses one of the most magnificent and grand festivals every year between March and April. The Arubathu Mūvar Utsava (festival of the sixty-three Śaiva savants) as it is known when the bronze images of all the sixty-three Nāyanmārs are taken out in sixty-three wagons around the four streets surrounding the huge temple tank.

Several *nāgasvaram* sets lead the procession along with musicians (*oḍuvars* singing hymns), folk dances like dummy horse, *karagam* (dancing with pots on heads), *kolāttam* (dancing with sticks), *oyilāttam* (folk dance) and *mayillāttam* (peacock dance).

At Thiruvarur during the Ādipuram festival (between 15 July and 15 August), the temple float is taken around the massive tank outside the temple thrice. The temple is known as "Kamalālaya". *Nāgasvaram* rituals, formatted especially for this festival, are followed to a great extent even today. When the float is taken around for the first time, the *peria melam nāgasvaram* artists perform. One of the main compositions they have to play is *śrī nīlotpala nāyakī* (the presiding deity in the temple built within the tank).

This song, set to tune in the Rītigaula Rāga, is one of the nine *kṛtis* dedicated to this goddess. They are composed by Muthuswamy Dikshitar (*fig.* 27) and it would be interesting to note that all the nine *rāga*s end with *gaula* like Kedāragaula. In the second round, the *chinna melam* artists get into the float. They will have to play Muthuswamy Dikshitar's *kṛti Kamalāmbike* set in Toḍī Rāga. This, again, is one of the nine special compositions dedicated to Goddess Kamalāmbā, the presiding deity and the consort of Lord Tyāgeśvara. In the third and final round, *oḍuvar*s get into the float and sing the prescribed hymns (*Tevarams*). While the *nāgasvaram* rituals continue to this day during the float festival, the dance performed by *devadāsī*s in the moving float alone does not happen. It stopped about sixty years ago.

The Taipūsam festival (December–January) is another festival wherein the deity (*utsava-mūrti*) is brought out in a chariot. As the deity is taken towards the chariot, the *nāgasvaram* artists should play the Pāras Rāga. From there to the eastern *gopuram* (temple tower) *mallāri* is played and then while proceeding to the four-pillared *maṇḍapa* (hall), a *padam* in Bhairavī Rāga followed by the beats in *ada tālam* is performed. Other prescribed numbers are — Śuddhaśavarī (*varṇam*), one or two *padams* in Dnyāsi Rāga and *tāla*s (*miśra tāla* and *tripuṭa tāla*). The trend of playing songs came later and were started by the Thiruppamburam brothers and followed by Madurai Ponnuswamy and the Thiruvizhimizhalai brothers.

We can say that the above concept (*paddhati* — formatting) can be compared to that of the contribution (the concert *paddhati*) of Ariyakudi Ramanuja Iyengar, the greatest Carnatic music vocalist of all times. This concert pattern formatted by Ariyakudi is practised by all musicians to this day.

Unique Nāgasvaram Traditions in Some Temples

In Thiruveṅgaḍu Śrī Aghoramūrti (Śiva Temple) near Chidambaram, there is a rule that Mohana Rāga should be played before *mallāri* in Gambhīra Nattai Rāga. It was considered that Mohana Rāga was exclusively meant for the presiding deity hence it was a taboo to play this *rāga* anywhere outside the temple, not even on weddings or other auspicious occasions. This is a ritual that is practised till today.

In the Vedāraṇyam (near Nāgapaṭinam) Temple very strictly formatted *nāgasvaram* rituals were observed. Early morning *pūjā* with Bauli Rāga, the next *pūjā* between 8-9 a.m. with Kedāram or Dhanyāsi Rāga, the noon *pūjā* with Śrī Rāga or Manirāṅgu Rāga, the evening *pūjā* between 5-6 p.m. with Kalyāṇī Rāga and at night only Begaḍa Rāga were played.

In Avudayarkoil (Śiva) Temple, *nāgasvaram* was played only opposite to the *sanctum sanctorum* near the *balipīṭha*. In Kutralam (famous for its waterfalls) the famous Kutralīśvarar Temple (Śiva) is situated and in Tenkasi, just a few miles away from Kutralam, the Arudra *darśana* is observed with big festivities. On the day of the above-mentioned festival, the *nāgasvaram* artist would first play the Ānanda Bhairavī in *ādi tāla* and then would continue the same in *miśra capu tāla*.

While the artist played the instrument, *arcaka* (priest) would bring *dīpa* (a decorative metal lamp) dancing to the beat of the music. This ritual would last for over fifteen minutes and other instruments that accompanied *nāgasvaram* were *śaṅkha, tavil, mr̥daṅgam, otthu* and *tālam*. This ritual is known as Tāṇḍava Dīpārādhanā and is observed late in the night. This ritual is still in practice, but *nāgasvaram* rituals have become more flexible. When I say flexible, mention must be made that during the days of the *devadāsī*s they performed the above-mentioned dance carrying the lamp. Today it has saturated or modified to the priest performing the dance.

In the Chidambaram Temple (*figs*. 28 and 29), the playing of *rāga*s and music forms by the *nāgasvaram* players had been formatted and it is to a great extent followed even today, particularly during festivals. On the first day of any festival only Ārabhi Rāga or Dhanyāsi Rāga is played. At night Śaṅkarābharaṇam is played. On the second day Rītigaula, third day Mayamalavgaula and fourth day Cakravaham are played. On the fifth day till the *utsava-mūrti* reaches the *vāhana* (carrier in which the deity is placed), a ritual called Tervadaithan takes place. *Nāgasvaram* is also accompanied by *nattumaṭhau* (a small *mṛdaṅgam* hung on the player's neck).

On the sixth day Ṣaṇmukhapriya Rāga or Toḍī has to be played, seventh day Kambhojī or Varali, eighth day the *odakara* (boatman) song in Nadhanāmkriyā Rāga will have to be played. On the ninth day — the day the temple car (*thera*) is brought to take the deity out — *mallāri* should be played.

When the deity reaches the *āyiramkāl maṇḍapam* (thousand-pillared hall) "*eccarika* songs" set in Ahīrī or Nīlāmbarī are played. These songs will have to be followed by anyone *padam* (dance composition) on the presiding deity Lord Naṭarāja. The *nāgasvaram* artists in this temple have been playing here for several generations and hence the rituals handed over to them continue even today to a large extent.

In Nañjanguḍ (Karnataka) Śiva Temple, everyday the temple elephant brings water from the Kabinī River about 100 m away from the temple. The priest sits on the elephant with a silver pot and is accompanied by the *nāgasvaram* artist and party during the entire ritual till the water is taken into the *sanctum sanctorum*.

In Tiruvannamalai every year, on 15 August, Śrī Aruṇagirināthar day is observed. Eminent *nāgasvaram* artists participate in the festival. At least, fifteen sets of *nāgasvaram* artists perform in this ritual. These *nāgasvaram* artists play in the four streets of the temple beginning in the night and conclude in the early hours of morning. All the sets perform *rakti* together first and then play a couple of popular *Tirupugazh* (composed by Aruṇagirināthar) and they break into individual groups and perform for the limited given time according to seniority. People throng the temple just to hear their favourite artists play *nāgasvaram*.

In Cheyur, situated on the East Coast Road between Chennai and Pondicherry, a very unique tradition of music was followed till the late 1950s during the Vasantotsava (spring festival) in March–April featuring several instruments to accompany seventy-two music rituals. Here too *nāgasvaram* had a significant position. Beginning with vocal presentation of hymns from *Tevaram* it used to get concluded with the *bhujaṅga nr̥tya* (snake dance). This unique form of worship that lasted for over four hours was known as *sarva vādya valipadu* (all instruments worship).

There were a lot of dancers who performed during this ritual. When the *devadāsī* system was abolished these rituals also came to a halt and thus many such unique and interesting music rituals have been lost or are slowly losing their identity in the temples while some still continue in a more modified manner. There are many elderly devotees living in the vicinity of the temple who visit the temple even today and are the only ones who can take us down the memory lane and rewind to us those glorious days.

Festivals at Thirumala

It is believed that Śrī Veṅkaṭeśvara enjoys festivals (*utsavas*) and therefore every moment in Tirumala (*fig.* 30) is considered a festive occasion. The most important festival is the Brahmotsava observed during Navarātri that occurs between 15 September and 15 October every year. This nine-day festival is a spectacular and grand in every respect.

Beginning with a flag hoisting (*dhvajārohaṇa*), the festival starts. *Dhvaja* (flag with the emblem of a black eagle, Garuḍa) is hoisted at the *śrīvari ālaya dhvajastambham*. The huge metal pillar on which the flag is hoisted is at the entrance of the temple. After the flag hoisting, the presiding deity Lord Veṅkaṭeśvara, in all His magnificence and majesty, is taken around the four streets of the main temple on the huge *pedda śeṣa vāhana* (big snake carrier) from 22.00 hrs till midnight.

Beginning from here everyday morning and night the deity is taken out in different huge carriers with the traditional *nāgasvaram* sets (many sets), vocal music, different dance forms, Vedic chanting, Āḷvār *pasurams* singing and so on.

On the second day, the deity is taken out on the smaller snake vehicle (*chinna śeṣa vāhana*) in the morning and in the evening on the swan vehicle (*haṁsa ratha*). On the third day morning the deity is taken out on the lion vehicle (*siṁhavāhana*) and in the evening on *mutalayapandan vāhana.* On the fourth day, the deity is taken out on the *kalpavṛkṣa vāhana* (the celestial tree) in the morning and in the night, it is carried on the *sarvabhūpāla vāhana*. On the fifth day, the Lord is dressed up as Mohinī and is taken out a palanquin (*pālakī*). Lord Kṛṣṇa is also taken out in the same procession. In the night, the deity is taken out on the *garuḍa vāhana*.

On the sixth day, the *hanumanta vāhana* procession is done in the morning and in the procession at the night, the Lord mounts on an elephant (*gaja vāhana*). The next day, in the morning, the vehicle is the *sūryaprabhā vāhana* (sun-shaped vehicle), and the deity is taken out in a procession in the night on the *candraprabhā vāhana* (moon-shaped vehicle). On the eighth day, the Rathotsava is celebrated amidst great fanfare and a lot of music, dance and folk arts, etc. accompany it. It is believed that those who witness the Lord being taken in His chariot will not be reborn.

rathotsavam keśavam dṛṣṭvā punarjanma na vidyate

People pull the chariot chanting Govinda, Govinda. In the

night, in the procession the deity is taken out on the *aśva vāhana* (horse vehicle) and on the ninth day, the entire festival concludes with the deity being taken on *pālakī*. After performing all the religious rituals (*abhiṣeka*) with auspicious ingredients like sandalwood paste, oil and milk, the Garuḍa flag is lowered to signal that the festival is over. Every night there is the *ūñjala sevā* (the deity is placed on the swing) — except on the six day when the Vasantotsava is celebrated — and devotees get a *darśana* while the swing is gently rocked to and fro to the music of *nāgasvaram*, after which the deity is taken back to the *sanctum sanctorum*.

All the nine days the rituals go on till midnight and there is no dearth of music in all its forms. *Nāgasvaram*, of course, plays a stellar role with the recitation of hymns from the Āḷvār poems (*pasurams*) from *Divya Prabandham* and songs of Annamācārya on Lord Veṅkaṭeśvara on *nāgasvaram* and also vocal.

This is just one of the few festivals celebrated at Tirumala. But year around festivals are celebrated not only in Tirumala but also in the Govindarāja Swamy Temple at the foothills of Tirumala and Thiruchanur where the presiding deity is Goddess Padmāvatī, the consort of Lord Veṅkaṭeśvara. Millions of people visit all around the year, participate in the festivals that offer music, divinity and spirituality, all in one.

Everyday there is Kalyāṇa Utsava (marriage festival) at Tirumala in the specially built wedding hall where devotees can celebrate the wedding of Lord Veṅkaṭeśvara and Goddess Padmāvatī. They are given the privilege of playing parents to the deities and perform the wedding with all the wedding rituals. Needless to say that *nāgasvaram* again is the centre of attraction, playing songs prescribed for weddings (*kalyāṇa-sampradāya*).

The Venkateswara University, which is affiliated

to Tirumala Tirupati, runs courses on *nāgasvaram*. The students and teachers of the musical courses there conduct a vocal and instrumental musical programme, called "Nāda Nīrañjanam", every evening for the devotees. In this too *nāgasvaram* has its place. Interestingly, Venkateswara University also boasts of having women lecturers in *nāgasvaram*. *Nāgasvaram* thus plays a predominant role in Tirumala Tirupati.

KALYĀṆA SAMPRADĀYA (PLAYING AT WEDDINGS)

In south India, particularly in Tamil Nadu, *nāgasvaram* is a must in all the weddings. Like all wedding rituals, which are considered sacred and have some significance, *nāgasvaram* too is considered sacred and auspicious.

A few decades ago people used to invite *nāgasvaram* artists according to their status to perform at the weddings. The artist would be required to play for one to two days and sometimes would be required to stay at the wedding hall if the timing was the early hours of morning. Those were the days when wedding dates were fixed up only after getting the confirmation from a popular *nāgasvaram* artist whose name will find a special mention in the wedding card (*fig*. 31). Nowadays *nāgasvaram* artists are available at the wedding hall on contract basis, so being a part of the contract they are employed by the wedding house, and are booked by the wedding hall authorities.

However there is not much change in the rituals, only timings are limited as people prefer more varieties to traditions as part of entertainment like dancing or singing of film songs like *antākṣarī* and so on. But *nāgasvaram* has to be played during the auspicious timing of tying the sacred knot and on other occasions that are parts of the wedding ritual (*figs*. 32 and 33).

In a wedding occasion, as a ritual, the artists sit on the

stage specially erected for them at a distance, from the *maṇḍapa* where the bride and bridegroom are seated. The previous day of the wedding, the *nāgasvaram* artist normally plays, for about one hour or more as an entertainment (concert) while people are arriving and taking their seats and getting ready to join a few rituals. The bridegroom then goes to the temple with all the family members in an open car. This ritual is known as *janavāsam* and is similar to *bārāta* in the north Indian weddings. *Nāgasvaram* leads the procession to the temple and the entire group returns to the hall and after some rituals they all break up for dinner.

The next day morning the *nāgasvaram* artist and party, at least an hour before the arrival of visitors, begin with the traditional morning Rāga Bhūpāla or Bauli followed by compositions of Saint Tyāgarāja in Mohana (mandatory), Kalyāṇī, etc. Then one by one the wedding rituals begin with the bride and bridegroom arriving and taking their respective places on the stage meant for them along with important members of their families and priests, and a few religious rituals take place.

When the bridegroom goes on the Kāśīyātrā with some relatives (a mock display), the *nāgasvaram* artist follows the little procession and comes back to take his seat on the stage meant for him. After this the bride and the bridegroom are brought out of the dais and made to sit on the swing and a few rituals take place like exchanging of garlands when the song *malai matrinaḷ* is played by the *nāgasvaram* artist and some other *ūñjala* (swing) songs are either sung by someone or played by the artist. Sometimes even the relatives of the bridegroom or bride will sing and the *nāgasvaram* artist accompanies them.

After other religious rituals the bride is given the traditional *muhūrtta sāṛī* by the parents. This is taken around the wedding hall along with the sacred thread to be tied.

Taking the cue, the *nāgasvaram* artist immediately switches over to Naṭakuriñjī Rāga and goes on playing it till the bride comes well ready for *māṅgalya dāraṇam* (tying of the sacred knot).

A few more rituals follow till the arrival of the auspicious time. The sacred thread is taken from the tray and handed over by the priest to the bridegroom. Meanwhile, another priest sends the signal to the *nāgasvaram* artist. There are a lot of *getti melam* signals from all sides. Generally there is a lot of noise and excitement in the air.

Getti can also mean strong or loud and *melam* is a cue for *tavil* who beats heavily followed by the *nāgasvaram* artist who quickly switches over to the Ānanda Bhairavī Rāga and then it is *ānanadam ānandam āndame* (happiness for ever) and this must be followed by the "Sītā Kalyāṇa Vaibogame, Rāma Kalyāṇa Vaibogame" (a recall of the wedding song of Lord Rāma and Sītā). After this they go on to play some popular songs. Of course, there are a few more rituals after the sacred thread is tied like *nalaṅgu,* after which the role of *nāgasvaram* is over in a wedding ceremony.

There are a few don'ts also in the wedding *sampradāya.* Some *rāga*s are considered not to be played or inauspicious because they denote *duḥkha bhāva* (sad feelings or emotions) like Varali, Mukharī, Ahirī Śubhapāṇḍuvarali and hence cannot be played. Even songs composed in *rāgamālikā* like Swathi Thirunal's *Bhāvayāmi* is not played to avoid the Mukharī Rāga in it.

NĀGASVARAM SAMPRADĀYA IN MAṬHAS

The *nāgasvaram* artists have been recognized by several *maṭha*s in Tamil Nadu for many years. Like the kings and *zamīndār*s, *maṭha*s also patronized them in a big way. As the *maṭha* heads in Tamil Nadu had the control of several temples (some still have it) for several centuries the *nāgasvaram* artists enjoyed the dual status of being recognized as *āsthāna vidvān*s of both the temples and the *maṭha*s. The Madurai *maṭha* and the Madurai temples (known as the Madurai *adhīnam*), the Dharmapuram temples and *adhīnam*, the Thiruvidaimarudur temples and *adhīnam* and the Kāñcī Śaṅkara *Maṭha* are a few to name. We find some artists keep the name of their *maṭha*s as prefix to their names.

The heads of the *maṭha* would come out to greet the devotees twice or thrice a day before or after visiting their temple to offer *pūjā*. During this time the *nāgasvaram* artists play moving with the *maṭha* heads who are accompanied by their disciples, office-bearers, etc. This little ritual is called *pattina-praveśam* (entering the town). They lead the procession and as a tradition, play only *kr̥ti*s (songs) composed by the Trinity. As a rule *rakti* or *mallāri* is not played.

NĀGASVARAM (CONCERT) SAMPRADĀYA

There is not much difference between a regular music (vocal or instrumental concert) though *nāgasvaram* concerts in temples differ a little from a stage concert.

Difference between Vocal Concert and Nāgasvaram

In a regular vocal concert the order is like this:

- Begin with *varṇa* in two or even three speeds (*kāla*s).
- One or two quick crisp and short *kr̥ti*s of commencing with a (Gaṇeśa *kr̥ti*) composed by Saint Tyāgarāja, Pattanam Subramaniam, Mysore Vasudevachar, etc. followed by *gāna rāga kr̥ti* by Tyāgarāja/Dikshitar, etc. in detail. The above *kr̥ti* is sung with an elaborate.
- *Rāga ālāpana* and then *neravaḷ*, followed by *svara*s. The whole presentation takes about twenty minutes. After another one or two crisp short *kr̥ti*s with a brief *ālāpana* or *neravaḷ*, *rāga–thāna–pallavī* is taken in detail.

- Again a small *kṛti* and then a *gāna rāga kṛti* in detail after which the percussion artists (*mṛdaṅga, ghaṭa, kañjira* and morsing) are given time to play *thānī āvarttanam.*

This is an item where the percussion artist or artists (one or more above said) will play all the technicalities for *tāla* of *kṛti* which the vocalist had just completed singing. *Kṛti* can be a basic *ādi tāla* or a *tripua* or a *jhampa tāla* — but the rule is that *thānī* should be played only in that *tāla.* At times the vocalist will have just one percussion artist (*pakkā vādyam*) to accompany him or her.

Sometimes there are two or more percussion artists (*upa-pakkā vādyam*) and then it becomes a more enjoyable one for the players who compete with each other showcasing their talents and also bringing out the best and complicated nuances in *tāla.* It is an enjoyable experience for the *laya* buffs.

Thānī also gives a little break to the vocalist and the violinist. After *thānī* that goes on for 15-20 minutes, the singer sings a couple of light songs like a *bhajana, pasuram* or *tevaram tirupugazh* before concluding. In a concert the rule is that no *rāga* can be repeated twice.

In an exclusive *nāgasvaram* concert, the concert pattern is a little different. The concert begins with a *varṇa* following which a couple of small *kṛti*s and one *gāna rāga kṛti* are taken in detail. But the difference is that in a *nāgasvaram* concert importance is given only to highlight *rāga*. So the *nāgasvaram* artist elaborates *ālāpana* and *neravaḷ* is not even taken up. Instead, the artist goes straight for *svara*s that follow *neravaḷ*.

Again *rāga–thāna–pallavī,* which is like a keynote to a vocal concert, has the artist singing in detail all the three. But in the *nāgasvaram* concert highlight is only on *rāga*. There is no *thāna* or *pallavī*. The *ālāpana* is followed by *rāgamaligai* (garland of different *rāga*s) *svara*s. *Rāgamaligai* is comprised of a minimum of three to nine or sometimes even fourteen *rāga*s.

The *nāgasvaram* artist presents a variety of notes (*svaras*) that are very structured in the most complicated manner. These *svaras* are known as *usi* (a term used for half beat count in *tāla* in *nāgasvaram*). It is also played in different speeds (*kālas*), and between the *nāgasvaram* artist and the *tavil* artist it is like a fast moving tennis match and needless to say that the sparkling *svaras* not only leave the players breathless but leave the audience equally spellbound and breathless in wonder. This exercise is presented in three *kālas* and is both *rāga* based and *laya* based.

These *svaras* are like jewels that adorn a deity, in the sense, adding more beauty to an already beautiful form. But more than that they are highly scientific and technical (mathematical, not easily comprehended by a layman). After this heavy and highly technical piece, the artists play some light items like a *Tevaram* hymn, a Purandaradāsa *kr̥ti*, or Bharathiyar song and conclude.

The *nāgasvaram* concert in a temple is a little more different. The *nāgasvaram* tradition lays emphasis more on the tune than the words (*sāhitya*). Thus a concert in the temple may begin with a couple of crisp songs and then go on to just one *rāga ālāpana* that will go on for as long as they want. The main artist may play the *ālāpana* for about twenty minutes and stop at a particular *svara* say *Pa* or *Da*. The accompanying *nāgasvaram* artist will begin from there and go on for about fifteen minutes and then again the main artist will start from where he stopped.

This enjoyable exercise is known as *mātu*. After this elaborate piece they start the *laya*-oriented challenging *svaras* that is already mentioned above.

4

Nāgasvaram in Other South Indian States

Nāgasvaram in Andhra Pradesh

Nāgasvaram enjoys the same status in Andhra Pradesh as it enjoys in Tamil Nadu with a few changes in traditions here and there. Some of the biggest and oldest Vaiṣṇava and Śaiva temples like Tirupati, Bhadrachalam, Simhachalam and Kalahasti are all in Andhra Pradesh, and pilgrims in thousands throng these temples throughout the year.

Chilakaluripeṭa is one of the most popular *nāgasvaram* schools of Andhra Pradesh and some very popular artists have been trained from there. The great composer Bhadrachalam Ramdass was born in Bhadrachalam and composed a number of songs on Lord Rāma, the presiding deity of Bhadrachalam. This composer also was an inspiration to Saint Tyāgarāja who composed many popular compositions in praise of Lord Rāma.

In Bhadrachalam, the Kalyāṇa Utsava (*figs.* 34 and 35) is observed everyday and hence *nāgasvaram* is played throughout the wedding rituals. Again the Śrīrāmanavamī festival (birth anniversary of Lord Rāma in the month of April) and other festivals follow some formatted *nāgasvaram* rituals.

The *nāgasvaram* artists of the Bhadrachalam Temple and temples around Bhadrachalam have been playing for generations and many of them are Muslims who have no discrimination to any religion. They play the instrument with the utmost devotion, dedicating their music to the presiding deity of whichever temple they have been attached to, for several generations. These artists had been given lands, monetary benefits, and also were *āsthāna vidvān*s of temples or the palaces of local kings in earlier times. They also served as cultural advisors and ambassadors to the *zamīndār*s and royalty.

Nāgasvaram features an important role in folk music and rural festivals in Andhra Pradesh. During the Makara Saṁkrānti (harvest festival in January) prayers are offered in open air to the Sun God in villages where the *nāgasvaram* music is mandatory. *Nāgasvaram* also plays a prominent role in dramas, street plays, folk music and sometimes in chorus singing (*bhajana sampradāya*).

Former chief minister, the late Rajashekara Reddy, had appointed many *nāgasvaram* artists as temple artists. They are appointed by the Hindu Religious Endowment Board and are treated as state government employees. A lot of temples have such artists performing. Traditions are not their priority, they play as per their given time schedule and as per their choice.

The Tirumala Tirupati Devasthānam runs the Venkateswara School of Nāgasvaram, affiliated to the Venkateswara University, Thirupati. This institute encourages *nāgasvaram* in a very big way. The students who study here are given stipend, free hostel facilities and also employment opportunities after they finish their course. Women are also encouraged to learn and teach. Smt. Easwaramma, Smt. Lakshmi Suvarna and Smt. Raniprabha are some of the lecturers in this institute, while Shri V. Satyanarayana heads the institute.

The wedding *nāgasvaram* traditions of Andhra do not

differ much from the wedding traditions of Tamil Nadu. While there is nothing mandatory they also have the privilege of playing as per their choice and playing film hits is a common feature — more to please and entertain the audience (the wedding guests).

According to a vocalist from Andhra, many vocalist-students seek the *nāgasvaram* artists for teaching them during their advanced stage of learning music. They approach these artists for getting trained in voice culture and also to enhance their voice towards strong and easy flow and also to cultivate the right kind of nuances in the notes of *rāgas*.

During the 1920s a famous *nāgasvaram* artist, Subbaiah Bagavathar, began a *sabhā* called Arya Gana Sabha where only *nāgasvaram* concerts were held. The Sabha comprised mostly of eminent Andhra Pradesh *nāgasvaram* artists as members.

Andhra Pradesh takes pride in having the most number of Muslim artists who have popularized the art in a big way and have also been the *āsthāna vidvān*s for several generations in these temples and continue to do so. Many of them are attached to major temples in and around Bhadrachalam and have been trained in the Chilakaluripeṭa paramparā and there are many women artists.

The Chilakaluripeṭa *paramparā* is connected to a number of temples where rituals like *ūñjala sevā*, *abhiṣeka* and *melukopu* are observed. In these temples mostly Bhadrachalam Ramdass's *kṛti*s are played. This school follows a very clean and refined structure giving utmost importance to the *sāhitya* according to Chitoor Leela Manohar Reddy, a vocalist and musicologist. *Mallāri* tradition is not mandatory in the Andhra temples like in the Tamil Nadu temples.

A few decades ago the *nāgasvaram* artists of Andhra were patronized in a big way by the *zamīndārs*, landlords and royal families like Bobili, Vijayanagara, Suluru, Nuzveedu and Panagal (Srikalahasti). There is perfect harmony among the Muslim artists and the devotees who come to the temple to worship and the temple authorities. Other than Tirupati and the Badrachalam Temples, we do not find formatted rituals in Andhra Pradesh temples nowadays.

WELL-KNOWN NĀGASVARAM ARTISTS OF ANDHRA PRADESH

Shaikh Madeena Sahib

He belongs to the family of *āsthāna vidvāns* of Śrī Veṇugopālaswāmy Temple at Krishnapuram in Visakhapatanam district. He had his training under Shaikh Chinnapeeru Sahib of Chikalapudi a village in Andhra Pradesh and his vocal training under one of the greatest musicians of Andhra Śrī Nedanuri Krishnamurthi. He is popularly known as Madeena Sastry.

Shaikh Mehboob Subhani and Kaleeshabibi Mehboob

Shaikh Mehboob Subhani was born in the year 1951 and his wife Kaleeshabi Mehboob was born in the year 1961. They are probably one of the very few husband and wife *nāgasvaram* duos of great repute (*fig.* 36). They belong to a large community of eminent *nāgasvaram* players who hail from Prakasam district. These artists have been attached to different temples in Prakasam district for several generations and play more for the commitment and love for their art than the remuneration. These artists do not have any discrimination in performing in the temples and when I visited some temples in this district for my other book *Music Rituals in Temples of South India,* I was overwhelmed at the way they spoke about the rituals and their benevolence towards the gods for whom they play, is something unbelievable. The music they offer for the presiding deity is the purest form of music coming straight from their hearts. Perhaps, it may be a constant reminder to us: "art is divine and it has no caste or creed barrier". Shaikh Mehboob Subhani had training under his father, who was an eminent artist of Andhra Pradesh. Shaikh Meeran Sahib and Kaleeshabi got trained under her uncle, Shaikh John Sahib.

They have also had formal training in the Kurnool Music College in Andhra Pradesh and later under the tutelage of the great Maestro Shaikh Chinnamoulana Sahib (*fig.* 37). They had gone to attend the Thiruvaiyaru Tyāgarāja Ārādhanā along with their *guru* K. Chandramauli. During the Tyāgarāja Ārādhanā festival there is an *ārādhanā* for Āñjaneya. This ritual is like an indication, bringing down the curtains of the big festival — the conclusion of the Tyāgarāja Ārādhanā.

A.K.C. Natarajan, the legend who headed the Tyāgarāja Aradhana Committee in 1981, asked the couple to perform for a short time before the commencement of the Āñjaneya Ārādhanā. The couple had not taken along their instruments, and when A.K.C. Natarajan offered them his instruments asking them to perform they were shocked with disbelief. To accompany them, they had senior *tavil* artists and the programme, though of a short duration, gave them a flying start in Tamil Nadu and there was no looking back since then. The couple is very popular and a much sought-after duo and are recipients of several awards and titles and have travelled a lot in the Gulf countries.

The Tenālī Couple

A popular couple Shri Venkateswarulu and his wife Smt. Hymavati have been performing for more than thirty-five years. They belong to the Tenālī Paramparā. They have travelled widely and have received several titles and awards.

Nāgasvaram maestro Thirucherai Swaminatha Pillai from Tamil Nadu regularly visited Tenālī and Kurnool and taught and trained many students who are performing in a number of temples all over Andhra Pradesh.

Nāgasvaram in Karnataka

Nāgasvaram plays an important role in temples and weddings in Karnataka as it does in Tamil Nadu but surely does not enjoy the same popularity it enjoys in Tamil Nadu because there are no strict rituals attached to this instrument in Karnataka. Yes, it is mandatory to have *nāgasvaram* in weddings and temples but it is more customary.

All big temples have the *nāgasvaram* artists playing once or twice a day and they are mostly appointed by the state government. This happens only in those temples that are affiliated to the Hindu Religious and Charitable Endowment Board. The artists are paid a monthly salary and they just have to play for a specified time.

There are many temples, particularly in the coastal region of Karnataka, where a lot of rituals are followed, especially in places like Udupi, Śṛṅgerī, Subramaṇia and Kolur. Here we do find a lot of music and a lot of these rituals were formatted by Ādi Śaṅkara several centuries ago. While many music rituals (traditions) have been stopped due to non-availability of artists, lack of interest by authorities and also fund constraint. However, rituals in the form of offering food, fruits, flowers and special *pūja*s and festivals dedicated to deities still continue. Festivals especially the Daśaharā is celebrated with pomp and posh. Music, dance, discourse and other folk art forms still continue and play a vital role in some temples, but some rituals particularly related to instruments like *mukha-vīṇā* are completely lost and rituals related to *nāgasvaram* have saturated to some extent.

Similarly in Mysore, and towns in and around Mysore where the *mahārājās* used to patronize art a lot, we find some changes in the rituals owing to time and fund constraints. It is surprising to note that many of Tamil Nadu *nāgasvaram* artists were honoured at the Mysore Palace and enjoyed a lot of benefits and privileges during the period of the Wodeyars in the early nineteenth century CE. Today *nāgasvaram* does not enjoy that kind of patronage anymore in Karnataka.

NĀGASVARAM IN TEMPLES OF COASTAL KARNATAKA

Some of Karnataka's oldest and famous temples are all situated in Coastal Karnataka. These temples observe a lot of rituals in the form of worship, music and so on. The rituals are more religious than cultural, and have been laid by Ādi Śaṅkarācārya and Madhvācārya (Udupi) and are all followed strictly to this day.

These temples attract a lot of pilgrims from all over the world throughout the year and it is a combination of three sects in Hinduism — Vaiṣṇavites, Śaivites and Madhvas. Some of the temples here are a must for the Hindus to visit at least once a lifetime. These temples are situated in and around Western Ghāṭs in picturesque valleys, mountains, gorgeous waterfalls and a trip to this place will serve a double purpose — that of a pilgrimage and of sightseeing. This is one place where one can worship God and Nature all at once!

In all the temples situated in the Coastal Karnataka, Navarātri is observed for nine days with a lot of pomp and grandeur, and equal importance is given to the classical arts and folk arts. Besides these, festivals like Gaṇeśa Caturthī, Kṛṣṇa Jayantī and Rāmanavamī keep alive all art-related rituals. These festivals offer classical music, dance and also ancient folk art *yakṣa-gāna* (a folk dance-drama), discourses, puppetry, group singing and so on. Thus along with worship, the pilgrims also get a cultural flavour of the typical coastal Karnataka arts.

Śrī Kṛṣṇa Temple, Udupi

This temple (*fig*.38) is the first among the seven important places of pilgrimages for the Vaiṣṇavites. The presiding deity Lord Kṛṣṇa is in the form of a little child like Guruvāyur Kṛṣṇa in Kerala. A very unique aspect about the temple is that the presiding deity Lord Kṛṣṇa can be worshipped only through the window with nine holes called *navagraha kiṭikī* (nine-housed window).

In the sixteenth century, during the reign of King Vādirāj, a devotee named Kanakadāsa, an untouchable, went to Udupi to have a *darśana* of Kṛṣṇa. Being an untouchable he was not permitted to enter the temple. Kanakadāsa broke into a song for Kṛṣṇa beseeching him to give His *darśana.* Lord Kṛṣṇa is believed to have created a small hole and turned His face the other side so that his devotee could get a glimpse of Him. This hole came to be known as "Kanakana Kiṇḍī". This poet composed hundreds of songs on Lord Kṛṣṇa like Purandaradāsa. These songs known as *Dasara Pada* are sung several times for the deity everyday as part of the music rituals of the temple.

Another unique feature about this temple is that this is the only temple where religious rituals are conducted fourteen times a day beginning from 4 a.m. to 11 p.m. The rituals here are very interesting and unique because the God here is a little child who is pampered by the devotees. He is dressed up as per the wishes of his devotees. Everyday he is dressed up in a different form. On Friday Lord Kṛṣṇa is in the form of Goddess Durgā. His devotees love to see Him bathed, cradled and rocked, made to sleep in a golden cradle with sweet lullaby music. He is offered varieties of sweets, savouries, rice and fruits, everyday. The devotees are kept on their toes because they have a demanding child to take care of.

Beginning with first *pūjā* that commences at 4 a.m. there are ten *pūjā*s till noon that conclude at 1 p.m. called as the *mahāpūjā*. In this *pūjā* a number of *prasāda*s (sweets, savouries, a variety of rice, fruits, curd, butter milk, etc.) are offered. *Āratī*s are offered after *naivedya* (food offering), amidst music dominated by *nāgasvaram* accompanied by a number of instruments like *śaṅkha*, *bherī*, *ghaṇṭā* and *tāla* for some time. Musicians known as the Bhāgavats sing devotional songs on Kṛṣṇa in groups and also dance. After the singing and dancing there is a lot of drum beat — *nāgarī* with *nāgasvaram* conveying to the entire town that the *pūjā* is over and it is time for the little Lord to relax.

Again at 4 p.m. the rituals commence and there are four *pūjā*s that conclude with the placing of Kṛṣṇa in the golden cradle rocking Him and singing lullaby. This ritual known as the "Śayanotsava" is followed by the *ekānta-sevā* (when the Lord enjoys His solitude) that happens at 11 p.m. but sometimes goes on till midnight. About a few years ago only *mukha-vīṇā* was played but now it has stopped completely. *Nāgasvaram* is played only during the main *pūjā* and the flute has taken over *mukha-vīṇā* or rather has substituted *mukha-vīṇā*.

Śrī Mañjunātha Temple, Dharmasthala

The presiding deity of this 800-year old temple on the bank of Netravatī River is Śrī Mañjunātha (Śiva). *Nāgasvaram* is played several times during rituals for long durations. Also it seven major festivals in a year: Gaṇeśa Caturthī, Navarātri, Dīpāvalī, Lakṣadīpotsava, Śivarātri, Annual festival and Tenth-day festival (14 May). A lot of *nāgasvaram* is heard in these festivals. The artists have been here for generations and follow certain standard patterns in playing the instrument.

Kollur Mūkāmbikā Temple

Famous shrine of Goddess Mūkāmbikā, believed to have been built by Ādi Śaṅkara, is situated here. This temple is well known for *vidyārambha*. *Nāgasvaram* is played for the presiding deity in the morning and evening, and Fridays and festive days when the deity is taken within the four walls or outside the temple.

Śṛṅgerī Śāradā Pīṭham

This houses the temple of Goddess Śāradādevī and follows religious, musical and other rituals formatted by Ādi Śaṅkarācārya (*fig.* 39). *Nāgasvaram* is played early morning to wake up the deity and once in the night. Every Friday evening and on full-moon days the instrument is played when the deity is taken around the temple (*prākāra*). Navarātri in this temple is a grand nine-day affair with performances of various art forms including *nāgasvaram*.

Kukke Subramaṇia Temple

This is a very ancient temple and the presiding deity is Lord Subramaṇia (*fig.* 40). *Nāgasvaram* is played here just once in the morning. The temple is situated deep inside the forest of the Western Ghāṭs and people from all over come here for getting rid of *sarpa-doṣa*.

Mysore Daśaharā

The Mysore Daśaharā is a ten-day festival that has been going on for centuries and even today it attracts tourists from all over the world like the Madras Music Season. The celebrations take place inside the Mysore Palace and the temples around. The ten-day Daśaharā procession abounds with music and dance. I shall only go into *nāgasvaram* details that have been going on for centuries.

The Mysore Daśaharā Festival Committee decides the *nāgasvaram* artists who would be invited to perform on the inaugural day and during the main day of the procession. On the inaugural day, the festival begins with *maṅgala-vādya*. One very eminent artist from Karnataka or outside is invited to perform a regular full-fledged concert in the Palace.

During the procession (*fig.* 41) that lasts for around ten hours, at least ten sets, comprising of at least twenty *nāgasvarams* and forty *tavils*, are invited to play in the procession. They all begin outside the palace and play for about half an hour in unison. Besides the *nāgasvaram,* Western bands (police band, etc.) also participate.

At a particular point the senior artists leave and the disciples take over to play till they return and join again at the time of concluding in the wee hours of morning. *Vīṇā* has always enjoyed the topmost priority in the Mysore Daśaharā celebrations and in the Mysore Palace for many centuries. This is because some of the greatest *vīṇā* artists have been born in this state and have promoted *vīṇā* in a big way like *vīṇā subbanna.*

Śrīcāmuṇḍeśvarī Temple, Mysore

This ancient temple built by the Wodeyars for the Goddess Cāmuṇḍā Devī is atop a hill with the palace situated at the foothill. For many years *nāgasvaram* has been a part of the ritual in the temple and is played four to five times a day beginning with the waking up of the deity and then midday, evening and at night when the deity is all set to get back to her *sanctum sanctorum* to sleep. *Nāgasvaram* is played in the silence of the night for about half-an-hour. The sweet melody (lullaby in Nīlāmbarī Rāga) of the *nāgasvaram* notes echo all around the hills soothing not only the Goddess but also Her devotees.

After the concluding day of Navarātri, the float festival and the Rathotsava are celebrated with the deity being taken out and *nāgasvaram* accompanying the deity in a grand manner.

The Nañjanguḍ Śiva Temple

An ancient and a big Śiva Temple (*fig.* 42) with a massive Nandī (Bull) situated about 20 km from the Mysore Palace. The Mysore Mahārāja used to visit this temple everyday in his horse-driven chariot from his palace, a tradition that was followed for a long time.

Nāgasvaram plays a predominant role in this temple. For every *pūjā* the instrument is played for at least half an hour. A unique feature in this temple is that every morning the temple priest sits on the temple elephant carrying a silver pot and goes to the nearby Kabinī River to fetch water for the deity's bath. The entire proceedings are done with the *nāgasvaram* artist playing the instrument and accompanying the elephant, as we have already seen.

The Śrīraṅganātha Temple, Śrī Raṅgapaṭnam

The ancient temple of Lord Raṅganātha, built by the Chozha kings, attracts a lot of devotees. Lord Raṅganātha is in the *śayana* (sleeping) posture on the five-headed snake with His consort Lakṣmī. There are three such temples — Śrīpadmanābhaswāmi Temple, Trivandrum, Śrīraṅganāthaswāmi Temple, Śrīraṅgam, and the Śrīraṅganātha Temple. There is a belief that if one is able to visit the three temples on the same day, one will get salvation. There are a lot of *nāgasvaram* rituals attached to this temple and followed to a great extent.

Bangalore Temples

Some of the very old temples with a lot of *nāgasvaram* rituals are found in one of the oldest parts of Bangalore,

Mallesvaram. One such temple is the "Kadu-Malleśvara" (forest) a very ancient Śiva Temple from where the name Mallesvaram is derived. The *nāgasvaram* artist attached to the temple plays regularly four times a day.

Another temple in Mallesvaram is the several hundred years old Śrī Kr̥ṣṇa Temple. In this temple, *nāgasvaram* is played four to five times a day for at least half-an-hour duration. The temple also conducts "Kalyāṇa Utsava" four or five days a week with the performance of *nāgasvaram* for the wedding rituals. Besides this there are a number of festivals beginning with "Janmāṣṭamī". In all the festivals the religious aspects and the *nāgasvaram* rituals are observed.

The poetess Āṇḍāḷ's (one of the twelve Āḷvār Vaiṣṇavite savants) birthday is celebrated in a grand manner and so is the last day of Makara Saṁkrānti when Āṇḍāḷ is taken in procession to the nearby Gaṇeśa's temple to keep the traditional Kannu. It is a festival like Rakṣābandhana in north India where sisters pray for the welfare of their brothers. The Gaṇeśa Temple, the Śaṅkara Maṭha, and the Rāghavendra Maṭha, all situated in Mallesvaram, have a lot of *nāgasvaram* music played regularly and during festivals.

The Bull Temple in Basawanagudi (temple of the Bull) has one among the five biggest Nandīs (Bulls) and is situated on a hillock in the city. The Nandī is known as God of *laya* and is supposed to play the celestial *mr̥daṅgam* for Lord Śiva.

Though listed among the *nāgasvaram* stalwarts of Karnataka, Rāmadāsappā deserves a special mention here. He is a great *nāgasvaram* maestro and a much sought-after artist in Bangalore. He has been attached to the temples mentioned above for over four decades. He is popularly in demand for weddings and has the unique distinction of having played in several families for the weddings of three generations. Rāmadāsappā is also considered as auspicious as his instrument.

WEDDING SAMPRADĀYA OF NĀGASVARAM IN KARNATAKA

Nāgasvaram is a part of the wedding rituals and in most of the weddings the artists are engaged for two days and sometimes for three days. *Nāgasvaram* is played during *varapūjā* (religious rituals performed to receive the bridegroom's parent and relatives the day before the wedding). The *nāgasvaram* artists wait in attendance and play as the bridegroom's party arrives at the wedding house. They play as they are received and garlanded by the bride's people.

In the evening, the *nāgasvaram* artists play for a while. This is more as an entertainment for the guests and then after some religious rituals the bridegroom and his relatives are taken to a nearby temple by the bride's relatives. The *nāgasvaram* artists also accompany the procession playing some pieces and again perform till they return to the wedding *maṇḍapa*. This ceremony is similar to *bārāta* in a north Indian wedding.

Nāgasvaram is played during the *muhūrtta* (tying the sacred knot) and rituals that follow before and after the marriage. It is also played (optional) during the *devara samārādhana* (special wedding feast) hosted by the bridegroom's party the day after the wedding. The *nāgasvaram* artist stays at the wedding hall seated on a dais specially erected for him to perform for the above rituals.

NĀGASVARAM STALWARTS OF KARNATAKA

Belluraiah (1900-71)

He was born in a village called Śāligrāma in Karnataka, then known as Mysore State, in a family with a rich *nāgasvaram* background. He was in the Mysore Representative Assembly (Hon.) and later was nominated as a Hon. Magistrate as a mark of respect for his artistry in the instrument. He founded the Sarada Sangita Pathasala at Holenarsipur.

K.V. Muniswamappa (1928) (*fig.* 43)

He was born in the year 1928 at Kundhanam and was a very famous artist. He was popularly known as "Kundhana Muniswamappa". He was attached to some important temples in Bangalore (East) city. He was the president of the Nāgasvaram Society for a long time. Many of his disciples are performing artists.

Nāgārāju (1892) (*fig.* 44)

His father was a *nāgasvaram* artist by name Chikka Narasiṁhayya. He was the disciple of the legend Thiruvalluputtur T.K. Venu Pillai. He was the *āsthāna vidvān* of the Mysore Palace and the recipient of several awards and titles.

B. Rāmadāsappā (1930) (*fig.* 45)

He was born in 1930 at Bangalore and is one of the most popular and famous *nāgasvaram vidvāns*. His *guru* was his father, an eminent *nāgasvaram* artist Chikka Muniswamappa. He has performed in many cities in India and abroad. Ramadasappa has received several titles and awards at state and national levels. He has been attached to the important temples of Mallesvaram for over thirty years. He is a senior grade AIR artist and has performed in the Doordarshan several times. He is a much sought-after artist for weddings and has the unique distinction of having played for three generations in several family weddings.

D.V. Venkatesaraju (1933-80) (fig. 46)

He was born in the year 1933 at Denkanikotte, a village near Hosur. He had his tutelage under stalwarts like Dassappa, Annamalai A. Govindarajan and A.V. Narayanappa. He has performed in several cities in India and overseas, and was a senior grade AIR artist and performed in the Doordarshan several times. A recipient of several awards and titles he was known as Nāda-Kokila, a title conferred on him by his admirers. He died in the year 1980.

Tavil Stalwarts of Karnataka

Karnataka has many *tavil* artists to its credit. They have accompanied *nāgasvaram* artists from Karnataka and other states. The most popular *tavil* artist is Denkanikotte R. Munirathnam. He not only accompanied many stalwarts of *nāgasvaram* outside Karnataka but also has the distinction of having accompanied *sitār* legend Pandit Ravi Shankar and the greatest flautist of all times T.R. Mahalingam, popularly known as Mali.

Nāgasvaram in Kerala

NĀGASVARAM TRADITIONS IN KERALA TEMPLES

Origin of the Instrument

It is widely believed by the people of Kerala that the name *nāgasvaram* originated because of the shape it resembles — a snake in some form. The other version is that it originated from Nagoor (Nagapattanam) in Tamil Nadu where the tribals called Naganmar used to play this instrument. Sometimes it is also pronounced as *nākasvaram* and in Malayalam *nāka* means world at large. In Kerala, a wood called *karinthali* or *acharam* is used to make the instrument.

Stone Nāgasvaram

Interestingly there are *nāgasvarams* made of pure stone

and these are still available in the temples of Vaikom, Ettumanur and Omallur in Central Travancore. These are not exhibited on a daily basis, but shown as special cases to visitors. This stone instrument, even though smaller than the present *nāgasvaram,* was in use in ancient times and thereby establishes the fact that *nāgasvaram* was a temple instrument used widely during the ancient period in Kerala. It will be interesting to note that the instrument can be played even now, though it is bit difficult to handle it.

Nāgasvaram is played in all the major temples of Kerala like Trivandrum, Guruvayur, Ambalappuzha (*fig.* 47) and Trichur. A lot of temples have *nāgasvaram* mostly known as *nādasvaram* and also called as *nākasvaram* in some places.

In Kerala, importance has always been given to percussion instruments and one always associates *chenda* and *pañca-vādyam* (the five percussive instruments). *Pañca-vādyam* is played in all the temples as a part of music rituals in Kerala. But *tavil* as an accompaniment to *nāgasvaram* is very rare or in some places not even heard of. *Nāgasvaram* is a must when the deity is taken out in a procession. Inside the temple Śrī Rāga and other major *rāga*s are played and in many cases *tavil* is totally absent for reasons not clear.

Moreover if it is a two-round procession, *nāgasvaram* will accompany the deity in both the rounds and if it is four or five rounds the instrument will follow for two rounds only, and percussive instruments comprising of *pañca-vādyam* like *chenda* and other temple instruments accompany the remaining rounds of *pradakṣiṇā* (going around within the four walls of the temple a few times).

Nāgasvaram is played only inside the temple but never when the deity is taken out. Only on some exceptions like the Āratu festival in the Padmanābhaswāmi Temple in Trivandrum (*fig.* 48) it is played in the procession.

Nāgasvaram is used in all the major temples of Kerala for the main *pūjās* conducted three or four times a day and common *rāgas* used are as follows:

Description	*Name of Rāga*
Early morning *pūjā* — when the deity is woken up between 4-4.30 a.m.	Bhūpāla, Revatī, Revaguptī, etc.
Uṣā pūjā — normally conducted after sunrise between 7-8 a.m.	Bhairavī, Śrī, etc.
Panthīradi pūjā — when the temple is closed by 10-11 a.m. In major temples like Guruvayūr and Sabarimala, the closure ceremony takes place between 11-12 hours or even later	Bilaharī, Kalyāṇī, Bhairavī, etc.
Dīpārādhanā-pūjā — evening around sunset 6.15-6.45 p.m.	Śaṅkarābharaṇam, Kalyāṇī, Darbār, Mañji, etc.

Vaikom Mahādeva Temple

In almost all the temples including Vaikom Mahādeva Temple, the *nāgasvaram* artist with the *tavil* player stands outside the main temple premises, near the flag staff and *balikaḷ* (sacred stone) where he plays for all the major rituals including *navāṅgam* (waking up of the deity), *sīvali* (procession in the morning), *uchapūjā* (when the temple is closed in the afternoon).

Nāgasvaram is again played for *dīpārādhanā* (evening *pūjā*) and finally *athāzha sīvali* (when the temple is closed for the day). Again it is a major instrument used when the deity is taken outside the temple for *ārattu*. *Nāgasvaram* is played for all the rounds, right through the year except for *śrī bhūtabali* (a major ritual conducted during the temple festivals) and for this ceremony only three rounds are taken by the *nāgasvaram vidvān* and the balance two rounds by the other temple instruments.

For *paḷḷiunarthaḷ* (when the deity is woken up early morning), normally a Bhūpāla *kr̥ti* is played and at Vaikom Temple it is Swātitirunaḷ's "Pārvatī Nāyaka", later all the major *rāgas* including Abherī, Mohana, Āradhi, Kalyāṇī and Śaṅkarābharaṇam are taken up. *Ādi tālam, rūpakam, miśrakandacapu* and other *tālams* normally used in Carnatic music are also used in concert programmes in Kerala. Traditional or pure *rāga vistāram* (elaboration of *rāga*) can be taken up only by a *nāgasvaram vidvān* and not by a vocal artist.

According to Murugadoss, a *nāgasvaram* artist from Kerala, from whom all the above information was gathered there is no authentic book that gives any information on *nāgasvaram* in Kerala.

Mullackal Mahādeva Temple, Thiruvizha

Nāgasvaram accompanied by *tavil* and *eḍakka* (percussion instrument of Kerala) is played at the Mullackal Temple (*fig.* 49) during the following *pūjās* inside the temple in front of Sreekovil.

Paḷḷiunarthaḷ	—	4.30 a.m. (wake up)
Uṣā pūjā with *sīvali*	—	7.30 a.m.
Uchapūjā with *sīvali*	—	11.30 a.m.
Dīpārādhanā	—	6.30 p.m.
Athāzha-pūjā	—	7.30 p.m.

Thiruvizhza is a small town, 20 km away from Alappuzha. There is a music institute at Vaikom (Kshetra Kalapeetham) which started functioning from mid-1950s and has around 200 students now, all hailing from all over Kerala. Apart from *nāgasvaram*, they teach Carnatic music, *tavil, chenda* and other temple instruments. Noted *nāgasvaram* players like the Ambalapuzha Brothers, Haripad Brothers, Thiruvizha Raghava Panicker (Jayasanker's father), etc. were attached to this institute during the last century.

In central Kerala there are not many *nāgasvaram* artists and so is the case in the Malabar region. In the Chittoor region, namely the Thattamangalam areas of the present Palakkaḍ district, we find a few artists.

NĀGASVARAM IN KERALA WEDDINGS

Nādasvaram is played as a *maṅgala-vādyam* for marriages and at times it forms a part of a concert programme. But when the knot is tied, the instrument is played for around five minutes, and Tyāgarāja's Utsava Prabandha *kṛti Sītā Kalyāṇam* (in the Navroz Rāga is commonly played in all the south Indian states after the nuptial knot is tied) is the favourite *kṛti* for all including the artist and family members.

WELL-KNOWN NĀGASVARAM ARTISTS OF KERALA

Ambalapuzha Brothers

Sankaranarayana Panicker (1911-67), Gopalakrishna Panicker (1914-76) and Ramakrishna Panicker (1917-82) (*fig.* 50) were three illustrious brothers who made *nāgasvaram* immortal in Kerala during the latter half of the twentieth century. Their father Vaikom Kuttappa Panicker was a famous *nāgasvaram vidvān* of his times and their mother Smt. Kuṭyammā, a *saṅgīta viduṣī*. Having born into a culturally rich household they have made contributions not just on the field of *nāgasvaram*, but also Kathakali, dance, vocal music and other ritualistic art forms.

The eldest of the brothers, Sankaranarayana Panicker, learnt from Chidambaram Vaidyanatha Pillai for one-and-a-half years. After this, he proceeded to learn from Tiruvidaimarutthur Veeruswami Pillai for seven-and-a-half years. Around this time the younger brother Gopalakrishna Panicker started his tutelage under the same *guru*.

The duo gave several performances in Tamil Nadu during that time with and without their *guru*. Recognitions sought out the brothers and their names became synonymous with *nāgasvaram* in Kerala. They received the title of *kīrtanālaṁkārabhūṣaṇa*, from the then *rājā* of Ramanathapuram. Later, the brothers also received the Kerala Sangeeta Nataka Academy award.

Apart from promoting their art form and teaching students in the *gurukula* tradition, the brothers used a lot of their wealth, made from *nāgasvaram*, to set up an academy of dance and music.

The Chembakassery Nadana Kalamandalam attracted the best of the teachers and the most enthusiastic of students then. No temple festival was considered complete without the Ambalapuzha Brothers accompanying the deity.

Ārattu (float festival) at Padmanābhaswāmi Temple (*fig.* 51), Aṣṭamī at Vaikom Mahādeva Kṣetram, Ettumānur Ezhara Ponnāna are only some of the annual events they were invited to participate every year. These are apart from the *nāgasvaram* concerts they gave at several temples in and around Kerala.

In spite of learning from *vidvān*s in Tamil Nadu, their style is slightly different from the one practised there. They brought in emotions of vocal music into the aspects of *rāga*, *kīrtana* and *svara*. This required them to learn the original lyrics of the song and understand the many layers of its meaning while learning a song, instead of just the notes as in the case of a musical instrument. Including a small element of *bhāva* while playing the *rāga* in a *kīrtana*, is another interesting aspect of their style. They also brought Kathakali *pada*s to the concert stage, thus bringing a new Malayalee approach to *nāgasvaram* presentation.

Sankaranarayana Panicker served the Kerala Sangitha Nataka Academy, during which he, along with Kavalam Narayana Panicker, brought about changes in the functioning of the organization. He has written extensively on music and other temple-related art forms.

Once when a journalist asked him if it is called *nādasvaram* or *nāgasvaram* he is known to have remarked "Neither, it is actually the *nākasvaram*". The brothers were also instrumental in bringing the first school to their village and they together put an end to the additional charges levied by the transport authorities on anybody who carried a musical instrument in a public bus.

The picture of Ambalapuzha brothers is incomplete without the mention of the youngest brother Ramakrishna Panicker (Ramunni). Being multi-talented, he was adept at Kathakali, dance, flute and the *chenda* apart from *nāgasvaram*. After the death of the eldest brother, he joined Gopalakrishna Panicker to continue the lineage of Ambalapuzha brothers. Their contributions to the society, especially in the field of arts make them an example for every artist to emulate.

Haripad Brothers

Haripad is a small town near Ambalapuzha and the famous Subramania Temple, known for its music festivals during Navarātri is its big attraction.

"Haripad Brothers" — K. Gopalakrishna Panicker and K. Chellappa Panicker — were maestros in the art of *nāgasvaram* in Kerala. They were born to Ambalapuzha Koyickal Kesava Panicker and Haripad Kottasseril Parukutty Amma.

K. Gopalakrishna Panicker was born in 1919 and K. Chellappa Panicker in 1924.

Their father was their first *guru*. He was an icon in *nāgasvaram*. He pioneered the introduction of "double *nāgasvaram*". He was the only artist from Kerala who was holding a *Thanka Nagasvaram* during his time.

The brothers later continued the training under *gurukula* system with *nāgasvaram* Chakravarthy Thiruvidamaruthoor P.S. Veeruswamy Pillai for four years. Their maiden performance was in 1941 at Vaikom Mahādeva Temple. They had performed throughout Kerala and other important places like Bombay, Delhi, Calcutta, Haridwar, Badrinath, Rourkela, Vrindavan, and Varanasi. They also performed several times in Sri Lanka. Their concerts were frequently broadcasted from Ceylon Radio Nilayam and Akashavani, Thiruvananthapuram Nilayam. They used to play comparatively longer *nāgasvaram*, known as *pari*. They were awarded with *thankapathakkams* (gold medals) and other awards and accolades several times by various organizations.

Karuvatta Brothers — Murugadas, Krishnakumar — Kalarcode Gopalakrishnan are a few among their eminent disciples.

K. Gopalakrishna Panicker lived in Alleppey. He died on 4 February 1995. K. Chellappa Panicker lived at his native place Haripad. He died on 31 July 1991.

Thiruvizha Jaishankar

He was born in 1937 in a village called Thiruvizha meaning "festival" in the Alappuzha district of Kerala. Thiruvizha is a little town situated between Alappuzha and Cherthala and has a very famous and ancient Śiva Temple known as Mullackal Temple.

He had his training under his father, a well-known *nāgasvaram* artist, Thiruvizha Raghava Panicker who had to his credit a number of awards and honours. Jaishankar was able to balance with ease his scholastic studies and his art, and was the first ever *nāgasvaram* artist to graduate with music and philosophy as his subjects in the year 1962.

His debut performance was with yet another famous maestro from Kerala, Ambalappuzha Sankaranarayana Panicker. A senior level artist in the AIR since 1965, he was deprived of the central government scholarship to pursue advanced training in that instrument as he was not willing to sacrifice his degree course. He has travelled intensively in India and abroad, and has a lot of discs and albums to his credit. One of the most popular artists, he also has several titles and won many awards.

Haripad V. Murugadoss

Born on 15 May 1971, Murugadoss is a Carnatic musician in the wind instrument *nāgasvaram*. A leading disciple of *nāgasvaram* maestro Thiruvizha Jaishankar, he is also a musicologist and the Head of the Department Kshetra Kalapeetham at Vaikom (Kottayam district). Born in Haripad, in Alappuzha district of Kerala, Murugadoss learned the basics of *nāgasvaram* from the great *nāgasvaram vidvān* late Haripad Chellappa Panicker and now learning and performing under the guidance of *nāgasvaram* maestro Thiruvizha Jaishankar. He is an A-grade artist in AIR, Trivandrum.

5

Great Nāgasvaram Maestros

FROM the early eighteenth century till now *nāgasvaram* has seen many great maestros who have left a huge legacy in the form of this divine art form. From the later half of the eighteenth century to almost the late 1960s this art form was at its zenith and the artists were treated with great regard and respect. This era saw the advent of magnificent *nāgasvaram* colossus who not only took the instruments to dizzying heights but also came to be recognized as the torch bearers of Carnatic music.

The *nāgasvaram* players had a huge fan following, patrons and were constantly in demand being invited for temple festivals, weddings, cultural and even political functions. They also were invited abroad and around the country — always a symbol of divinity and auspiciousness. We can assertively say that this period was the "golden age of *nāgasvaram*".

Many artists in this period have contributed their lot and have left their strong imprint by way of concert patterns, temple traditions, wedding traditions, teaching methodology and so on. "*Nāgasvaram* is an instrument which has human whims and fancies" according to a musicologist. "It is attuned to the mood of the player in a sympathetic rapport."

Nāgasvaram has a hypnotic effect that it liberates the higher mind from the physical limits of physical form. It is an instrument between the will of God and the will of man.

Nāgasvaram till the beginning of the twentieth century was only a part of the traditional temple music rituals. But thanks to the great performance of such artists it became an instrument with a distinct identity in the domain of Carnatic music. These artists also helped in raising *nāgasvaram* to the status of a mainstream musical instrument.

Another great development was that the instrument, that strictly belonged to Tamil Nadu and reflected the Tamil culture, not only spread out to the entire south but also to the overseas, particularly to Sri Lanka, Malaysia, Singapore, and even Australia, and now enjoys the same status it enjoys in the south Indian temples.

Many of the artists during this era went to Sri Lanka, Malaysia, Australia and Canada — places where the Indian settlers (Diaspora) built temples. They have settled there and have taken this art only to develop it in a big way and have given *nāgasvaram* a similar status symbol in the temples there also.

Just a few decades ago these artists were considered as status symbols and were in good demand to play at weddings and other functions. This was a time when the instrument enjoyed an indispensable and a mandatory status throughout festivities and was considered to be very auspicious and religious. Today, *nāgasvaram* does not get the recognition that it had a few decades ago.

The art may be having a little setback but the divinity and the role it plays in the religious, social and cultural activities remains much the same. Like in many of the traditions that have been followed, there have been compromises here and there. But it cannot be replaced by any other instrument or art in any way.

N. Rajagopalan, the author of the *Biographical Dictionary of Carnatic Composers and Carnatic Musicians* titled *Garland, Another Garland and Yet Another Garland* in English had been requesting the Tamil Nadu government and prime institutions to issue an order to make mandatory that all government functions should commence only with the rendering of *nāgasvaram*. After a lot of persuasion, the Tamil Nadu government relented and issued an order.

Through government order, permanent no. 329, Information and Public Relations, dated 23 December 1993, the Tamil Nadu government issued an order that henceforth all government functions would begin with the *maṅgala-isai*, thereby giving the art and the artist recognition in a candid way.

The book would go voluminous if all these artists are listed out. Hence I am listing out some very great maestros who have contributed something unique and also some artists who have left a great legacy for others to follow.

We find in the topography of this art and the villages that have given birth to some of the greatest *nāgasvaram* artists are all mostly from the Kāverī banks of Mayiladuthurai, Tiruvizhimamalai Tirumarugal, Keeranur, Injikudi and so on. We will hence find that most of these artists are from places in and around Thiruvarur and Tanjavur. The artists are listed in an alphabetical order for easy reference, and the order has nothing to do with their skill and fame.

Chidambaram Vaidyanatha Pillai (d. 1937)

He was an exponent in *rāga–thāna–pallavī* and was also known as Pallavi Vaidyanatha Pillai. He was a contemporary of Semponnarkoil Ramaswamy Pillai and had training along with him under Koorainadu Natesa Pillai.

His performance before the *jīra* (*maṭha* head) of Vanamamalai in the year 1925, where he had taken up Varali elaborately, has created history and is still spoken about in the music fraternity. His accompaniment on *tavil* on that occasion was Ammapettai Sri Pakkiri Pillai.

Chidambaram Radhakrishna Pillai (*fig.* 52)
(Interviewed at *Sampradāya* on 27 July 1986)

His father Swaminatha Pillai was an established artist and was attached to the Chidambaram Temple. His *guru* was Guru Thirukannamamalai Sundaram Pillai. He began playing *nāgasvaram* from the age of twelve. He later studied under Chidambaram Vaidyanatha Pillai for many years. He became the *āsthāna vidvān* of the Chidambaram Temple when he was twenty-seven years old and remained so till he breathed his last.

T.P. Girivasan
(Interviewed at *Sampradāya* in 1985)

He was the *āsthāna vidvān* of Vaideeswaran Temple near Chidambaram. The deity Lord Vaidīśvaran (Śiva) is the healer of all diseases and it is believed that bathing in the huge temple tank in this temple after worship cures one of all ailments. Hence the temple attracts millions of people right through the year. T.P. Girivasan is both a *nāgasvaram* and *mukha-vīṇā* artist. His father was his *guru*. He used to play more of *mukha-vīṇā* than *nāgasvaram.*

T. Govindaraja Pillai (1914)

He came from a family that had been the *āsthāna vidvān* of the Mayuranathar Temple for several years. His maternal grandfather was an eminent Bharatanāṭyam exponent.

Injikudi Pichaimuthu (1903-75)

Injikudi Subaraya Pillai was a great Bharatanāṭyam exponent. His sons Namasivayam, Kumaraswami and Narayanaswami were reputed *nāgasvaram* artists of their times. Pichaimuthu was the grandson of Narayanaswami and enjoyed a very privileged status in the *nāgasvaram* fraternity at a time when it was studded with great luminaries of the art. Son and disciple of Kandaswamy

Pillai, later the disciple of the maestro Koorainadu Natesa Pillai, he came to be popularly known as Injikudi.

Injikudi had received many titles and honours and was honoured as the court artist of Trivandrum and Mysore palaces. He used to give concerts on the AIR from the day of its inception.

Injikudi Brothers (E.P. Ganesan and E.P. Kandaswamy)

Sons and disciples of Injikudi Pichaimuthu, they were later trained by their uncles Thiruppamburam Meenakshi Sundaram Pillai and Sivasubramaniam Pillai. They have toured extensively in and out of India and have been recognized with several titles and awards.

Karukurichi Arunachalam

Born at Karukurichi in Tirunelveli district he made his debut when he was just eleven years old. He began his vocal training under Kalakad Ramanarayana Bhagavatar and *nāgasvaram* under his father and later intensive training under the tutelage of the great legend T.N. Rajarathnam Pillai.

He was known for his melodious rendition of the instrument. His style of rendering the instrument gave stress and importance to soothing melody, mass appeal and captivating delivery and presentation. A very popular classical number played by him as an accompaniment to a vocal recital by a female vocalist for a Tamil film became a great rage among music lovers and also set a new trend of *nāgasvaram* — voco ensemble (combination).

He died prematurely when he was at the zenith of his career about eight years after the death of his *guru* leaving a void never to be filled. He was honoured with many awards and titles.

Keeranur Brothers

Sivasubramaniam Pillai (1891–1942) was born at Keeranur a village in Nannilam taluk, Tanjavur district. Kannappa Pillai (1897–1944) was born at Sirupuliyur near Pandanallur, a village famous for dancers. The two were not brothers but destiny brought them together in the name of *nāgasvaram*.

Sivasubramaniam Pillai, also known as Chinna Thambi Pillai (*fig.* 53), had his initial training under his father Pallavi Govinda Nainakarar who was the *āsthāna vidvān* of Chunambedu Zamin. He later underwent training under his maternal uncle Swaminatha Nayanakarar at Kāñcīpuram. During his stay at Kāñcīpuram he had the great fortune of learning vocal music under the great legend Naina Pillai. And thereafter he retained the name Chinna Thambi Pillai.

After his training, he returned to Keeranur and continued his training under Keeranur Muthu Nayanakar whose son was the son of Keeranur Shri Ramaswamy Pillai, a lecturer in the Carnatic music College of Madras.

He became the regular *nāgasvaram* player at the Śivapurī Temple in Keeranur and also started giving performances outside Keeranur regularly. At one such concert he met Kannappa Pillai at Sirupuliyur and together they played at the wedding of *nāgasvaram* player Thiruvidaimarudur Veeruswamy Pillai.

The debut concert of these two players became the talk of the town and overnight they became a popular duo. Then and there they took a new identity as Keeranur brothers and thus began their career with a flying start. They were the honoured *nāgasvaram* players of many temples, *maṭha*s and kings and were given several awards, titles, etc.

Their much remembered and talked about concert is the one they performed in the year 1927 at the All India Music Conference held along with the All India Congress Committee session at Madras that was attended by many leaders like

Mahatma Gandhi, Netaji Subhas Chandra Bose and others.

Chinna Thambi Pillai was a fine vocalist and also a *tavil* artist and had accompanied many great *nāgasvaram* artists of their times. There were many occasions when he had a vocal concert in the morning and a *nāgasvaram* concert in the evening or vice versa.

When he died T.N. Rajarathnam brought a special commemoration to condole his death. Some of the great *tavil* stalwarts who accompanied the Keeranur brothers were Karaikal Palanivel Pillai, Needamangalam Meenakshisundaram Pillai, Nachiarkoil Raghava Pillai and many others.

Some of their very famous disciples were Vedaranyam Vedamurthy Pillai, Ambal Ramachandra Pillai, Seerghazhi Thirunavukarasu who later settled in Jaffna, known in Tamil as Yazhpanam, and Yazhpanam Ambulingam Pillai.

According to many of their contemporaries particularly *nāgasvaram* players, the two players never had any ego issues and there was a perfect harmony, and unison and perfect synchronization in their performances.

On 3 March 1942 when Chinna Thambi Pillai died, Kannappa Pillai had a mild heart attack and was not even able to attend the funeral. He never recovered from the attack and finally succumbed to it on 13 July 1944.

Kottai Subbaraya Pillai (1849–1919)

He was the son of Kottai Sundaram Pillai under whom he undertook initial training. The prefix "Kottai" is the Tranquebar-Dutch Fort built by the Danish in the seventeenth century CE, known in Tamil as Tarangabadi, few kilometres away from Mayiladuthurai.

He later underwent training under Thiruvarur Palanivel Pillai in vocal and *nāgasvaram*. His disciples were Chidambaram Vaidyanatha Pillai, Semponnar Ramaswamy Pillai and Koorainadu Natesa Pillai, who became great maestros themselves.

Kottur N. Rajarathinam Pillai

His first teacher was his grandfather Kottur Soundaraja Pillai but later he had his tutelage under the formidable Thiruvengadu Subramaniam Pillai from 1946.

Kuzhikarai Pitchaiappa Pillai (1913-79) (*figs*. 54 and 55)

He was born at Kuzhikarai, a hamlet in Tiruvarur district. He learnt under the tutelage of his uncle Perumal Pillai. Initially he played with Kalidasa Pillai but later began performing solo. His rendition of compositions (*kr̥tis*) echoed vocalist style. He was very popular for his soul-stirring presentation of *rāga-malikās*.

He was the *āsthāna vidvān* of Thiruvavaduturai Maṭh. He received the gold medal award Akhila Bharata Nagaswara Chakravarthy from the former Prime Minister Lal Bahadur Shastri in 1962.

Kuzhikarai S.P. Viswalingam (1926)

He belongs to the Kuzhikarai *paramparā,* a family of great *nāgasvaram* artists. He was the son of Kuzhikarai Pitchaiappa Pillai, grandson of Thiruvengadu Subramaniam Pillai and the nephew of the legend T.N. Rajarathnam Pillai.

Kumbakonam Sivakozhundu Pillai (1838–1911)

He was the *āsthāna vidvān* of the Kumbakoṇam temples. Played on the stone *nāgasvaram* in the Kumbakoṇam Temple as a challenge and won huge prize money from the *rājā* of Tanjavur.

Latchappa Pillai (1930–2013)
(Interviewed on 30 November 1986 and 24 April 2010 by M.A. Bhageerathy)

He belonged to the legendary family of the "Tanjavur Quartet", the direct disciples of Muthuswamy Dikshitar. The Tanjavur Quartet has contributed a lot to Carnatic music in the forms of dance, music, *nāgasvaram* and has also composed several *varṇa*s, *pada*s and *javali*s that are popular even today and performed by the dancers and vocalists.

These legendary figures were also patronized by Mahārāja Swāthithirunāḷ of Kerala. In fact, they have left a very rich legacy in the field of art that will remain popular in the entire southern hemisphere for ever. Latchappa Pillai who passed away this year (2013) had accompanied some of the greatest stalwarts like T.N. Rajarathnam Pillai, Thiruvengadu Subramaniam Pillai, Kuzhikarai Pitchappa and others. He was the nominated director for all the music colleges of Tamil Nadu till his death.

Latchappa Pillai belongs to the first *nāgasvaram* family that migrated from Thiruvarur to Tanjavur during the reign of the Emperor Rājarāja Chozha. This family is believed to have performed before the emperor and brought forth rains in the drought-hit Tanjavur at that time and were gifted an ivory *nāgasvaram*.

Today this *nāgasvaram* is with his family and is in the safe custody of a bank. It was brought for display and also was demonstrated by T. Latchappa Pillai in 2011 during an exclusive interview with *Sampradāya*.

Madurai M.K.M. Ponnuswamy Pillai (1879–1929)

He was the son and disciple of the very eminent *nāgasvaram* artist M.K. Muthukaruppu Nagaswarakarar from the family of the renowned Madurai school of *nāgasvaram* players. Having lost his father at the very tender age of five, Ponnuswamy went on to become the disciple of his elder brother M.K.M. Ayyaswami Pillai, the court musician of the Ramnad Prince. He was a much sought-after player and remained the court musician of the Raja of Mysore for many years.

Perhaps he was the only one to author a book *Poorveega Sangitha Unmai* (The Ancient Truth About Music — a literary translation). This he wrote to establish that *melakartā* (principal) *rāgas* are only thirty-two and not seventy-two as declared by the great musicologist of the olden times Venkatamakhin. He was a highly respected and revered member in the Experts Committee of the Music Academy, Madras.

Madurai Smt. Ponnu Thayi

A proficient and prolific player from Madurai she managed to remain popular in a male-oriented and dominated profession. This very popular lady artist was the disciple of Natesa Pillai, Ramaiah Pillai and Selvaratinam Pillai whom she had accompanied several times. She has travelled in and out of India and has given several performances.

Madurai M.P.N. Sethuraman (1928) and Madurai M.P.N. Ponnuswami (1933)

Popularly known as the Madurai Brothers, they are the grandsons of the above maestro. Their *guru* was their father M.P. Natesa Pillai and later M.P. Shanmugam Pillai, their uncle. When we mention great artists like these in this art form it is a very strange, surprising and a remarkable feature to note that a number of them were siblings!

They were recognized for their contribution by way of titles, awards and so on by their patrons, music lovers and the government. They also have travelled far and wide. Their popularity also reached greater heights in a different field — film — when a very popular novel based on a *nāgasvaram* artist was made a movie. The story was a serial, centred around a *nāgasvaram* player that was published in a popular Tamil magazine.

The film had the *nāgasvaram* artist and his music as the theme hence had the brothers rendering the instrument throughout the film. Their rendition of the instrument in the film got them a huge fan following.

Mannargudi Chinna Pakkiri Nayanakarar
(1869–1915) (*fig.* 56)

According to many eminent *nāgasvaram* players and *nāgasvaram* fans he was recognized as *na bhūto na bhaviṣayati* because of his mastery over the instrument. He began as an *otthu* player and then went to the great Mannargudi Veeraswami Pillai and played the *otthu* for him for some time for a salary of Rs. 21. After a short spell he went to Uraiyur with the saved money to learn under the tutelage of the great maestro Muthu Veerswamy Pillai following the *gurukula* system.

Here again he could not continue for long because of the heavy household chores given by the womenfolk. He ran away one night from his teacher's house and in his haste took some other person's instrument by mistake.

He landed up in a small town Needamangalam and continued his lessons under Guru Needamangalam Sivakozhundu Pillai and began to perform at the Needamangalam Temple. Slowly and steadily he became a popular artist and his music began to attract a lot of music lovers.

By sheer co-incidence his wife's name was Pakkiri Ammal and his *tavil* accompaniment's name was Pakkiriswamy. Once in a village called Ambal near Mudikondan town there was temple festival. Chinna Pakkiri had Pakkiriswamy on *tavil*. It looked as if they were made for each other being wizards in melody and rhythm, respectively. Chinna Pakkiri started to play the Begaḍa Rāga after the brief *mallāri* at 10 p.m. He went on playing the Begaḍa oblivious of the time and so was the crowd. When he finally concluded, it was noticed that he had played the *rāga* for more than three magic-filled, mesmeric hours. He then went on to a *rāga–thāna–pallavī* rounded off with *rāga*s Varali, Bilahāri and Kedāragaula. The deities returned back to the temple around 8 a.m. fully conscious of the fact that Śiva, Viṣṇu and Brahmā attained their full glory and personification through the *nādopāsanā* of the *nāgasvaram* maestro.

There are a lot of interesting anecdotes about this legend and other players too. I am mentioning a few only for readers to recognize the adoration and adulation these great maestros enjoyed those days. We also come to know the mutual respect the artists had for each other.

The deputy collector of Mannargudi was an ardent fan of Chinna Pakkiri. He was transferred from Mannargudi and on his last day of his service at Mannargudi he wanted to listen to Chinna Pakkiri. That evening during the Perumāḷ *vīdhi ula* (the deity's procession on the street) Chinna Pakkiri played his favourite Begaḍa Rāga for more than two hours while the content collector left for his new destination. Pakkiri Pillai finally went home feeling uncomfortable but was happy that he fulfilled his *rasika*'s wish. He died the very next morning.

One of his very popular students who made it big was Mannargudi Keeranur Kannappa Pillai (of Keeranur Brothers). Kottur Rajarathnam Pillai was his adopted son as he did not have any issue.

Nagapatinam Venugopala Pillai (1861–1917)

He was born in Tirukuvalai and was the son and disciple of Rakti Veeraswami who settled in the port town of Nagapatinam in Tanjavur district. He later underwent *gurukula-vāsa* from Saveri Kandaswami Pillai of Keevalur.

Venugopala Pillai was a staunch Śiva devotee and would never perform in any place that did not have a shrine nearby. He was an exponent in *svara* presentation and *rakti*. He remained the *āsthāna vidvān* of the Chidambaram Naṭarāja Temple till he died. He was the first *nāgasvaram* artist to perform overseas (Singapore). He took Needamangalam Minakshisundaram Pillai who was only twelve years old at that time to accompany him on *tavil*.

At Chennai (Madras then) he and Semponnarkoil Sri Ramaswamy Pillai performed at the Cennakeśava Temple and were presented golden *nāgasvarams* in appreciation of their performance.

Sarabha Sastri used to address him fondly as the *eka śānta grāhī* (one who masters on a single hearing).

Namagiripettai Krishnan (1924)

A well-known and very popular artist of the century, Krishnan learnt the instrument under his father Kannan and later went for advanced training under Arupukottai Ganesan from the age of fourteen. His brother accompanied him on *tavil* while the other brother Murugan was his co-player.

He did travel world over and was an honoured artist of the Tirumala Tirupati Devasthānam. He has been honoured with many titles including "Inkuzhal Isai Arasa", "Nagaswara Isai Mannar" and "Peunguzhal Pulavar Mani" and a Doctorate (an honour very few *nāgasvaram* artists have been conferred upon).

Pandanallur Ayyakannu Pillai (1868–1944)

Pandanallur is synonymous to the oldest and most authentic school of Bharatanāṭyam. It is also the home of some of the greatest stalwarts in *nāgasvaram*. Ayyakannu Pillai was noted for his long and continuous duration of rendering on the instrument. He was attached to the ancient Paśupatīśvara Temple at Pandanallur.

Pandanallur Guruswami Pillai (1875–1963)

He had his initial training under his father Viswanatha Pillai. Later in his eleventh year he learnt under Ayyakannu Pillai. He started performing when he was seventeen years old. He was unique in his rendering of *pallavī*, and in presenting subtle and sparkling *svara* permutations and combinations.

Ammachathiram Kannuswamy Pillai, Pandanallur Maragatham Pillai and Thirukadaiyur Chinnaya Pillai were some of the *tavil* maestros who had accompanied him.

Pandanallur T.R. Dakshinamurthy Pillai

He came from a family of very eminent *tavil vidvāns*. His grandfather was Maragatham Pillai a great *tavil* maestro and father Ratnam Pillai who was the court musician of the Mysore Palace for a long time. A unique and interesting fact about Dakshinamurthy Pillai is that the initial stands for *tavil* and R for his father's name Ratnam. His brother T.R. Muthappa Pillai was a *tavil* maestro.

Yet another interesting fact about Dakshinamurthy Pillai was that coming from a lineage of great *tavil* maestros he was the only one to take up *nāgasvaram* and did not undergo any formal training. It was more self-taught and he had admirers from his own fraternity who always mentioned his name when questioned as to whose *nāgasvaram* they liked the most. This not only included his contemporaries but also his seniors.

He was a much sought-after artist overseas, particularly in Sri Lanka, and his fans made it mandatory to have his concert during the Kadirkamam Murugan Temple festival in Sri Lanka. Almost all the great *tavil* maestros have accompanied him. Yazhpanam Padmanabhan, the famous *tavil* maestro, was his father's disciple.

Semponnarkoil Paramparā Pallavī

SEMPONNARKOIL RAMASWAMY PILLAI (1880–1920)

Many villages and towns were synonymous with an artist or the art itself. In the case of Semponnarkoil it became synonymous with the *nāgasvaram* as some of the greatest stalwarts of this art form hail from this little hamlet near Myladuthurai a town known for temples in Tanjavur district of those days.

Semponnarkoil is to *nāgasvaram* what dance is to Pandanallur. Both have the reputation of having contributed respectively to *nāgasvaram* and dance — the most authentic and the purest form of art.

Ramaswamy Pillai (*fig.* 57) was the son of Pallavi Vaidyanatha Pillai who was also his *guru*. Later he took the tutelage of the formidable Koorainadu Natesa Pillai. He was the court musician of Mysore, Trivandrum, Ramnad, Singampatti Udayarpalayam, Singampatti, etc. Ramaswamy Pillai was the recipient of several titles, awards and gifts like the Golden Nāgasvaram, Golden Thodas (bracelets) and Makarakandigai.

SEMPONNARKOIL S.R. RAJANNA PILLAI AND
S.R. SAMBANDAM PILLAI
(Interviewed at *Sampradāya* in 1986 and in October 2010 by B.M. Sundaram, percussionist and musicologist)

They (*fig.* 58) are the fourth generation to play this instrument and were in the zenith of their career till the late 1980s. S.R. Sambandam Pillai passed away recently and S.R. Rajanna Pillai does not perform owing to old age but nevertheless he still gives lecture demonstrations and was recently invited to The Cleveland Tyagaraja Aradhana in the US and felicitated and was also honoured by the Sangeet Natak Academy (Ministry of Culture, Government of India, New Delhi) earlier in 2013.

The music fraternity is indebted to such great families and artists for leaving behind such a great art and heritage which will have to be preserved in every way. Just honouring the artists with titles or awards is not enough but we must take up the art to their expectations with the same passion and dreams.

They improvised the *rakti melam* and also brought in *manodharamabānī* in *rāga ālāpana* and *pallavī* rendition for which they became trendsetters.

The Semponnarkoil Sampradāya has left a legacy (Pallavī tradition) to the *nāgasvaram* fraternity, thanks to the great effort of Semponnar Ramaswamy Pillai whose father Pallavi Vaidyanatha Pillai was an exponent in *pallavī* presentation. He had introduced a lot of innovative complexities (technicalities) in the rhythm patterns that are followed by the *nāgasvaram* artists of today.

The *tavil* artists those days would find it a challenge to accompany them particularly in the *pallavī* rendering that would go on even for more than three hours. When Semponnar Pallavi Vaidyanatha Pillai was alive only one *tavil* artist dared to accompany him — Thirukadaiyur Chinnaya Pillai.

The Semponnar *nāgasvaram paramparā* has contributed a rich legacy to the art and many disciples to carry over their traditions. This *nāgasvaram* family was honoured by in all the palaces, courts, *maṭha*s and temples all over south India and received several titles and awards not only in India but world over — Australia, Canada, Malaysia, Singapore and Sri Lanka, more recently in the Cleveland Tyagaraja Aradhana Festival.

Padmasri Shaikh Chinnamoulana Sahib

(Interviewed at *Sampradāya* in January 1993)

He was born in Andhra Pradesh in Karavadi, was the son of Kasim Sahib. He began his training under Adam Sahib, a famous artist from the village Chilakaluripeṭa in Andhra, which was noted for its special *bānī* (method) as the Chilakaluripeṭa *bānī*.

Chinnamoulana later relocated to Tamil Nadu first to Nachiarkoil, a village near Kumbakoṇam known for the ancient and famous Viṣṇu Temple and also for sculptural art in bronze. He came here mainly to study the Tanjavur *bānī* of playing *nāgasvaram*. Here Chinnamoulana underwent training from eminent *vidvāns*, the Doraikannu Brothers of Nachiarkoil. He became a great celebrity of his times and was awarded some of the most prestigious awards and titles not only in India but also overseas.

He was the (Hon.) Professor in the Government Music College of Thiruvaiyar for a long time. He had dedicated himself completely to the art and has founded the Saradha Sangeetha Ashram to teach the art under the *gurukula* system at the famous temple city Śrīraṅgam where he resided till his death in 2000. His sons and grandsons are all artists.

Thiruppamburam Brothers

Natarajasundaram and Sivasubramaniam, popularly known as the Thiruppamburam Brothers, were born in a village, Thiruppambaram. They belonged to a family of *nāgasvaram* artists and hymnodists. They had their vocal training under Umayalpuram Doraiswamy Iyer and Sathanur Panchanada Iyer, two well-known and popular musicians of those times.

Thiruppamburam is considered as a sacred village by the music fraternity and it has been a hometown for several artists besides dramatists and other musical forms. Ādiśeṣa, the deity after whom the village must have derived its name, is worshipped here and has been personified by many Tamil poets and saints.

Great *nāgasvaram* stalwarts like Swaminatha Pillai, a disciple of Koorainadu Ramaswamy Pillai, are other stalwarts who hail from the same village.

The Thiruppamburam brothers were known for their mastery over the *kr̥tis* (compositions) of Muthuswamy Dikshitar and Saint Tyāgarāja. The elder brother published Muthuswamy Dikshitar compositions (*Dhikshitar Kirtanai Prakasikai*) in the year 1904, as a tribute to the great composer. The younger brother's sons became famous *nāgasvaram* teachers at Annamalai University, Swamimalai and Palani music schools.

THIRUPPAMBURAM BROTHERS AND THEIR CONTRIBUTIONS

The two brothers have contributed immensely for this art and are remembered even today. Before the advent of these famous brothers, *nāgasvaram* was played only by one person. They were introduced together on the day of their debut and began performing together. In their very first concert they seemed to have impressed the audience with their superb performance. Their rendition always highlighted melody and was so appealing that people would throng in hundreds to listen to them.

The unique experience of listening to the duo's *nāgasvaram* concert attracted the music lovers so much that it caught the fancy of other players who started looking around for another partner (player), brother or no brother, to play with them as a co-player (not an accompanist).

Thus the brothers set the trend of the *nāgasvaram* duet which continues to this day. If playing a *rāga* for several hours in the instrument developed pristine heights, the credit again goes to the duo. They would begin performing late in the night and go on till early dawn sometimes playing just one *rāga.*

For many days people would be speaking about their rendering of a *rāga* that flowed gently all through the stillness of the night keeping both the gods and music lovers mesmerized and completely under their spell. People never felt boredom in listening to a *rāga ālāpana* for hours together when these brothers played. Time just seemed to stop when they began and the clock began again to tick only when the *rāga ālāpana* would finally stop. So this was another feather on their cap!

They were also the first to introduce playing of compositions of Muthuswamy Dikshitar and Saint Tyāgarāja in their concerts. Thus they became trendsetters in many ways and were also known as trailblazers with so many firsts among the *nāgasvaram* fraternity.

Thiruvaduthurai T.N. Rajarathnam Pillai (1898–1956) (*fig.* 59)

He was born at Thiruvaduthurai and his name became synonymous with the instrument or vice versa. His father was Kuppuswami Pillai. He had his initial training under Thiruvaduthurai Markandam Pillai and later from his uncle the legend Thirumarugal Natesa Pillai who later adopted him. He had rigorous vocal training under yet another stalwart of those days Thirukodikaval Krishna Iyer.

It is said that the sound and melody that emanated from his instrument was like magic — it could work like a lullaby to a crying baby, like a sedative to a person writhing in pain, and soften and silence a seething man in anger.

There was no one to surpass him in rendering of the Toḍī and the Ṣaṇmukhapriya Rāga according to the music lovers who still go nostalgic about it. Gramophone records of the late 1940s and early 1950s still take us back to the mesmeric magical Toḍī and Ṣaṇmukhapriya.

His presentation of *rāga*s covered the entire gamut, nuances and technical music intricacies, and all the shades and subtleties that there has been no one to this day to surpass him. He became a household name in Tamil Nadu and all days were auspicious thereby making his fans who would listen to his music either in the radio or on the gramophone, the two popular machines that played his music constantly. He revolutionized the art by taking in *tānapūrā* instead of *otthu* to substitute *śruti* (drone), and *mr̥daṅgam* instead of *tavil*.

This created a magic in his performance by making it a mellifluous melody. Thus the muffled sweetness of the otherwise loud instrument had the audience and music lovers spellbound proving the Tamil saying *magudyill kattunda nāgam pol* (like a cobra that is possessed by the snake charmer's tunes and is unable to move).

Awards, merits, medals, titles came by dozens and he was awarded the Padma Award in the year 1952. Being a very handsome-looking man he also did a movie *Kavi-Kalamegam* as the hero.

When the greatest *nāgasvaram* maestro died the funeral took place in Madras. The cortege covered the distance from Adayar to All India Radio on the Marina Beach. T.N.R.'s recorded music was played all through the funeral procession. It was quite unusual; because one never associates death with *maṅgala-vādyam.*

For a *nāgasvaram rasika,* he could associate *nāgasvaram* only with the eternal music of T.N.R. As an appreciation of his contributions to the art the Tamil Nadu government has built an auditorium in his name (*fig.* 60) and a number of music festivals and concerts are held there.

Thiruvengadu Subramaniam Pillai (*fig.* 61)

He was born at Thirnangur in the year 1906, a very sacred and special place for Vaiṣṇavites where the festival in honour of one of the great Vaiṣṇavite savants Thirumangaui Āḷvār is observed for forty-eight hours, non-stop. His *guru* was his own father Paramanantha Nagaswarakarar and his forefathers were great masters in *nāgasvaram.* He lost his father when he was only twelve years old. Hence he had to go to Thiruvengadu to his uncle Thiruvengadu Swaminatha Pillai under whom he continued his training. His repertoire was enriched vastly by Thiruvengadu Swaminatha Pillai.

His close association with the vocalist legend enhanced his knowledge in music. He began his career initially by accompanying his brother-in-law the legend T.N. Rajarathnam Pillai and then went on to become one of the greatest artists of his times.

His mentor was Chidambaram Vaidyanatha Pillai from whom he acquired the mellifluence in rendering which made him adopt *tambūrā* instead of *śruti* to the accompaniment of violin and *mr̥daṅgam.* He was the first person to perform (solo) a concert with these newly-introduced instruments (rather an experimental and revolutionary concert).

Nāgasvaram accompanied by the violin and *mr̥daṅgam* became possible only with Subramaniam Pillai's personal stature and made the music fraternity accept this experimentation as a concert format. He was the first *nāgasvaram vidvān* ever to be conferred with a Doctorate by the Tamil University, Tanjavur for his mastery over the instrument.

His rendition of *maguḍi* (snake-charmer's notes) had won him a huge fan following. He was also well versed in *kañjira* (percussive instrument) and many a time had accompanied Madurai Somu, a leading vocalist in the 1960s. Subramaniam Pillai had travelled widely in India and overseas and was the first *nāgasvaram* artist to receive the Fellowship Award from Sangeet Natak Academy besides many titles and awards.

He was an artist who belonged to those days of status-conscious families who believed in grand marathon weddings. These families even rescheduled their weddings to fit in with his busy concert schedule. Today he is remembered in the music circles for his contribution in raising the *nāgasvaram* to the status of a mainstream musical instrument.

Thirucherai Muthukrishna Pillai (1892–1929)

He began as a *tavil* artist and later switched over to *nāgasvaram*. A highly talented player and a wizard at *kṛti* rendition and *pallavī* exposition, he did not get the due credit that he rightly deserved and died at a young age.

Thirucherai Sivasubramaniam Pillai (1927-94)

Thirucherai T.V.S. Sivasubramaniam Pillai was born on 16 May 1927 and belonged to a family of musicians. He learnt his first lesson in vocal music from his grandfather Thiruppampuram S. Natarajasundaram Pillai and *nāgasvaram* from his father T.V. Subbaraya Pillai. He also learnt vocal music from his father-in-law

Sangeetha Kalanidhi Thiruppampuram T.N. Swaminatha Pillai and from a great vocalist of Chidambaram, T.N. Sivasubramaniya Pillai.

He had specialized in performing *kṛtis* of Thyāgarājar, Dikshitar and Śyāma Sāstrigal, and the Tamil compositions of Muthuthandavar, Gopalakrishnabarathi, Periyasamithuran, Bharathiyar and Bharathidasan, with *sāhidya-padantaram* in a beautiful style of his own.

Great *tavil* maestros who accompanied him were Needamangalam Meenakshisundaram Pillai, Thirumullaivoyil Muthuveeru Pillai, Nachiyarkoil N.P. Raghava Pillai, Kumbakonam K.A. Thangavelu Pillai, Needamangalam S. Shunmugavadivel, Thiruvazhundur Ramdoss, Yazhpanam Dakshinamoorthy, Valangaiman Shunmukha Sundram Pillai, Vadapathimangalam V.N.G. Dakshinamoorthy, Inivil Chinnaraja Vakerganesan, Valayapatti A.R. Subramaniam, Haridvaramanagalam A.K. Palanivel, Thiruvalaputhur T.A. Kaliyamurthy, Thirunelveli Nynarswamy, Thirupati Muniramaiah, Tenkanikottai Munirathinam, Thiruvidaimaruthur Venkatesan and Thirunageswaram T.R. Subramaniyam.

He has trained hundreds of students in *nāgasvaram* in Andhra Pradesh, Sri Lanka, Karnataka, Malaysia and Singapore. He has been a recipient of many awards and titles. Pillai passed away on 13 May 1994.

Thiruvizhimizhalai Brothers

Thiruvizhimizhalai is a celebrated Śaivite centre and has given birth to several *nāgasvaram vidvāns*. Subramania Pillai was born in the year 1895 and his younger brother Natarajasundaram Pillai in the year 1900. They had the *nāgasvaram* training under their father a famous *nāgasvaram vidvān* A.R. Swaminatha Pillai and vocal training under the Carnatic music stalwart Konnerirajapuram Vaidyanatha Iyer.

They lived and basked in the glorious times of other

celebrities and great legends like T.N. Rajarathnam Pillai, P.S. Veeruswamy Pillai and Thiruvengadu Subramaniam Pillai.

These brothers were responsible to elevate the status of the *nāgasvaram* artists and were the first office-bearers of the Tyaga Brahma Sabha at Thiruvaiyaru from the year 1933 a recognition given to them as a tribute to their eminent stature among the musicians.

They were in the prestigious Experts Committee of the Music Academy, members of the Tamil Nadu Iyal, Isai Nataka Manram, member of the Mayiladuthurai Municipality (Hon.), a symbol of recognition for the art indeed. They were the recipient of several awards and honours including the Sangita Kalanidhi Award of the Music Academy Madras in 1957.

Another "Thiruvizhimizhalai Brothers" — S. Govindaraja Pillai and S. Dakshinamurthy Pillai — initially had vocal training under their paternal uncle and later *nāgasvaram* training under their father Natarajasundaram. They were the *āsthāna vidvān*s of Dharmapuram and Thiruvaduthurai *maṭha*s and were attached to the beautiful Thiruvizhimizhalai Temple. During the peak of their career they travelled all over Sri Lanka. They received many awards and also bore the title "Nāgasvara Ratnam".

Thirumarugal Natesan (1900)

He was born at Thirumarugal into a family of *nāgasvaram* players, Natesan attained dizzying heights with his mellifluous performance and matchless artistry.

As an artist, he was acclaimed, for his superb and scintillating presentation of *rāga*s, particularly Kaṇāda, Atana and Sahana. These *rāga*s played by him found an aesthetic brilliance in his performances according to his *rasikas*. Natesan and his contemporary, the one and only flautist of his times Sarabha Sastri, were mutual admirers of each other and attended each other's concerts. Like Sarabha Sastri who died when he was just thirty-five, Natesan also died young at the age of twenty-five when he was at the pinnacle of fame and glory.

Thirumeignanam Natarajasundaram Pillai (1926-81)

He was a *pallavī* exponent and disciple of his uncle Narayanaswamy Pillai. He accompanied Thiruvarur Vaidyanatha Pillai for a long time before going on to solo performance. He was conferred *nāgasvara yaman* — artist who annihilates all other *nāgasvara* players.

Uraiyur Gopalswamy Pillai (1876–1917)

He was born into a family of some eminent *nāgasvaram* artists. Gopalswamy was the son of Uraiyur Muthuveeruswamy Pillai. He is believed to have been highly knowledgeable in theory too and hence was asked to write the foreword for Madurai Ponnuswamy Pillai's book *Poorviga Sangitha Unmai* (which contradicted Venkatamakhin's theory of the seventy-two *melakartā rāgas*). As he was not agreeable to Ponnuswamy's contention, he refused to write the foreword.

Sangita Kalanidhi P.S. Veeruswamy Pillai (1901-73)

Also known as Perambalur (his birthplace) Veeruswamy Pillai, he learnt *nāgasvaram* from his father P.V. Sundaram Pillai and later from Sivakozhundu Pillai (*fig.* 62) and Venugopala Pillai (*fig.* 63). He also learnt vocal under the great maestro Naina Pillai. He had accompanied many stalwarts like Semponnarkoil Ramaswamy Pillai, Thiruvidaimarudur Sivakozhundu Pillai, the greatest maestro Thiruvaduthurai Rajarathnam Pillai and other great artists of his times.

He was the *āsthāna vidvān* (honoured) of the Thirumala

Tirupati Devasthanam, Trivandrum Palace, Cochin Palace and temples like Villiputhur Āṇḍāḷ Temple, Nachiar Temple and honorary artist of *maṭhas* like Thiruvaduthurai and Darmapuram. He travelled all over India with his concert. He was awarded the Sangeet Natak Akademi award by the President of India in 1966 besides several titles and awards.

Famous among his disciples were Thiruvidaimarudur P.S.V. Rajamanikam Pillai and Ambalapuzha Sankaranarayana Panicker. He was conferred with the "Sangita Kalanidhi" award by the Music Academy in the year 1961. Many of the above-mentioned artists have had students performing world over and spreading the rich fragrance of this divine instrument. Here, we have to mention a few artists from the West. Charlie Mariano was one of the few Westerners who had the privilege of listening to *nāgasvaram* for the first time during his visit to Malaysia in 1960. He learnt *nāgasvaram* during his stay in India under M. Muthaiah Pillai, mastered the art, and has also the achievement of training a performer. His disciple is Tim Price at Berkeley in the US.

Roland Shaeffer, a German saxophonist, is another *nāgasvaram* artist who was trained under *nāgasvaram* artist Karupaiah Pillai from 1981-85.

Some Tavil Maestros

1. Ammachathiram Kannuswamy Pillai (1869–1923) — He was popularly known as *laya brahma*. He had accompanied great maestros of his times like Thirumarugal Natesan, Semponnarkoil Ramaswamy Pillai and the greatest flautist of all times Sarabha Sastri. Most popular among his disciples were T.N. Rajarathnam Pillai, Sangita Kalanidhi Mudikondan C. Venkatram Ayyar. He was a composer, vocalist and a *ḍholaka* player.

2. Ammapetai Pakkiriswamy Pillai (1874–1920).
3. P.N. Angappa Pillai (1889).
4. Haridvaramangalam Palanivel (1948) — He was trained under his father Thirucherrai Muthukumaraswamy Pillai. He is one of the most popular and sought-after artists of today having been awarded with several titles. He has performed world over and has accompanied other instruments like mandolin and saxaphone.
5. Karandai Shanmugam Pillai (1915) — He was the permanent *tavil* accompaniment to the great Mannargud Packiriswamy Pillai.
6. Illupur Panchami Pillai (Thirucherai Perumal Temple *āsthāna vidvān*).
7. Malaikottai Govindaswamy Pillai (1879–1931).
8. Mayandi Pillai — He was the *āsthāna vidvān* of the Pudukottai Palace. He had great many vocalists as his *rasika*s (admirers).
9. P.L. Natesa Pillai (1899).
10. Nachiarkoil Raghava Pillai — He had accompanied great *nāgasvaram* maestros of his times.
11. Needamangalam Meenakshisundaram Pillai (1894–1949).
12. Peruppallam P. Venkatesan (d. 1921) — He was the disciple of Nachiarkoil Raghava Pillai, and Talaichangadu Govindaswami Pillai. He played for *nāgasvaram* legends like Tiruvaduthurai T.R. Rajarathnam Pillai, Semponnarkoil Ramaswamy Pillai, Karukurichi Arunachalam and many other senior artists.
13. Thirucherai Muthukumaraswamy Pillai.

14. Thiruvalaputhur Kaliyamurthy.
15. Thiruvalaputhur Pasupathiaiya Pillai (1879–1958).
16. Thirukandiyur Balu.
17. Thiruvizhimizhalai Dakshinamurthy Pillai (1923).
18. Valangaiman Shanmukha Sundaram Pillai.
19. Vallayapatti A.R. Subramaniam.
20. Vazhuvur Muthuveera Pillai (1888–1922) — He was the only *tavil* artist to have been conferred the prestigious Sangita Kalanidhi Award by the Music Academy in the year 2009.
21. Porayar Venugopal Pillai — He was the grandson of *kiḍi-kiṭṭi* player Thillaiyadi Srinivasam Pillai. Created a contrivance to ease the burden of *tavil* players by introducing belt with which the *tavil* could be hung around the shoulder of the player. He has accompanied almost all the *nāgasvaram* stalwarts like Semponnarkoil Brothers, T.R. Rajarathnam Pillai, Thiruvengadu Subramaniam Pillai and many others. The ninety-six-year-old legend teaches at the Kovilur Mutt near Karaikudi and was recently felicitated for his contribution.

Landmarks in Nāgasvaram

- Semponnarkoil Ramaswamy Pillai was the first *nāgasvaram* artist to break **rpm records in a year**.
- Mahārājā of Mysore requested Maha Vaidyanatha Iyer to sing *pallavī* for Simananda *tāla* 128 *akṣaras*. Nobody was willing to play *mṛdaṅgam*. Pasupathikoil Veerabhadra Tavilkarar agreed to play and matched Maha Vaidyanatha Iyer with ease. Both received accolades and awards by the Mahārājā and the music lovers at his court. Thus was introduced a new combination followed by others like the legend

T.N. Rajarathnam playing to the accompaniment of *mṛdaṅgam*, etc.

- Thiruvengadu Subramaniam was the first *nāgasvaram* artist to be conferred with a Doctorate by the Annamalai University.
- Thirucherai T.V.S. Subramaniya Pillai had the unique opportunity of performing for a Bollywood movie in the year 1975 for a song composed by the famous yesteryears music director Shankar Jaikishen when he accompanied Asha Bhosle on his *nāgasvaram* for a song.
- Madurai M.P.M. Ponnuswamy was a highly knowledgeable person in music leading him to author a book in Tamil *Poorviga Sangitha Unmai* (*Ancient Truth in Music*) the first in the history of *nāgasvaram* by an eminent *nāgasvaram* artist himself.
- The Music Academy always inaugurates the Academy music season with the *maṅgala-vādyam* on the first day and a full *nāgasvaram* concert on the first day of the fifteen-day programme from the day of its inception some seventy-five years ago.
- The Brahma Gana Sabha in Chennai has been observing a ten-day *nāgasvaram* festival in January for the past six years. This festival is observed immediately after the music festival in Chennai and attracts the *nāgasvaram* lovers in large numbers. This festival is aimed at showcasing *nāgasvaram* artists from all over south India and honours both the *nāgasvaram* and *tavil* artists in the most befitting way.
- Smt. Madurai Ponnuthayi was the first lady *nāgasvaram* artist to perform in public.
- *Nāgasvaram* maestro Vyaswarpadi Kothadaraman was honoured by Kalki Krishnamurthy Memorial

Trust in 2013. He took the music fraternity by storm in 2012 by mustering a congregation up of thirty-five *nāgasvara vidvāns* and twenty-five *tavil vidvāns* and had them performed at the famous Shanmukhananda Sabha in Mumbai.

- Eminent *nāgasvaram* maestro A. Murugathas of Jaffna is the son of Arumugam Pillai. His father was the disciple of Kuzhikarai Kalidass. Murugathas, who shifted from Jaffna to Singapore Mariamman Temple, has now taken Canada by storm. Temples in Canada, which had recorded *nāgasvaram* music played during *pūjā* and festivals now, have artists going and staying there on contract basis for three years and playing at temples. They play (two sets) the traditional *mallāri* on special days and festivals, and also play daily for the regular *pūjās*. Weddings in Canada also have live *nāgasvaram,* thanks to the effort of Murugathas. A one-day *nāgasvaram* festival is organized in Canada by him and happens in Chennai too and is co-ordinated by Vazhuvoor Ravi, an artist from the lineage of famous legendary dance maestro of Vazhuvoor Ramaiah Pillai of the Vazhuvoor Sampradāya School of Dance. Vazhuvoor is a small hamlet about 5 km from Mayiladuthurai. One of the eight *virattanaṅgals* of Lord Śiva — temples marked with gallantry of Lord Śiva — is located here.
- Valayapatti Subramaniam organizes a Valayapatti festival in Chennai every year during the music season and honours artists from the music fraternity and conducts programmes.

Conclusion

UNTIL a few decades ago, temples gave equal importance to worship and art. The artists who performed in the temples gave priority to their art and were focused on promoting their art. To them their art was something handed over to them by their forefathers and it was their duty to preserve it for posterity. They also felt that they were the chosen ones by God and deemed it as their duty to perform before the gods and goddesses. They did not look for publicity or remuneration. There was a genuine concern and effort to preserve the art as they considered it as sacred.

Sadly, today, with the advancement in science and technology, there is a lot of time constraint. Many art forms are dying slowly. Lack of funds and interest, changes in the socio-cultural backgrounds and Western influences are perhaps some of the reasons why we are left with no more than a few inscriptions to convey the heritage of many temples.

Let us take a moment to look back and admire the devotion and conviction of the Āḷvārs and the Nāyanmārs who travelled long distances even to (north India) at a time when transportation was unheard of. What these savants have achieved is humbling, especially when mankind takes everything for granted.

Temples not only taught religion but also tolerance, appreciation of art, protection of environment, and socio-economic and cultural awareness and adjustments. Many artists, whose family was playing *nāgasvaram* for generations, have slowly shifted to other professions which are more lucrative. Several of the *nāgasvaram* artists and temple officials, with whom I had spoken to during this study, felt that the lack of a system for archiving these rituals will leave the future bereft of cultural heritage.

There were suggestions that a light and sound show or documentaries in the old temples could give the common man an insight into the glorious past of these temples. Many *nāgasvaram* players have not put the next generation into their profession. Until a few years ago, *nāgasvaram* concerts were in plenty during the music season. Nowadays only few *sabhā*s inaugurate the festival with *nāgasvaram*. Due recognition or monetary benefit is not given to these great masters so as to continue playing at their own initiative.

Media can play an important role here in recognizing the artists and the temples they perform in. Awareness among the citizens that temples were not only places of worship but also a centre for culture and social activities will go a long way in preserving our socio-cultural heritage. Apart from being rich sources of information for the history of India, they are also celebrated as a tourist's delight because of their architectural beauty. Preserving our temples and temple music will not only enhance the nation's economic standing but also give us a chance to relive the past.

Nāgasvaram is so much a part of our culture and one cannot imagine any auspicious event without the music of this instrument. In south India, particularly in Tamil Nadu, *nāgasvaram* is celebrated as much as a festival. Every Divālī begins with a *maṅgala gaṅgā snānam* (auspicious Ganges bath — every household will have preserved Ganges water in small urns that will be opened and added with the water before a bath). Divālī also begins with *maṅgala-*

isai (auspicious music) of *nāgasvaram*.

Before the advent of television, All India Radio (AIR) used to broadcast *nāgasvaram* music early in the morning at 4.30 a.m., a programme titled "Maṅgala Isai". Every household would have this music played in full blast. In villages and even in towns till a few decades ago, *nāgasvaram* artists would come home and play early morning and accept whatever was given to them.

Poṅgal or the harvest festival is another festival when the *nāgasvaram* artists in villages accompany the livestock on the day of the Mattu Poṅgal. They go from house to house, play the instrument and are honoured by the villagers.

Nāgasvaram hence plays a significant role in our festivals and celebrations. To every Indian the marriage ritual is significant and symbolic, the sanctity of vows is sacred. To this day, all the rituals in the marriage are followed and a marriage without *nāgasvaram* is unheard of. Like *sāta pherās*, in the tying up of the sacred thread, and other wedding rituals, *nāgasvaram* also is a part of the sacred rituals. These rituals have been going on for several generations and will never change. A constant reminder is needed that the roots of our culture and heritage are too deep that they can never be uprooted or compromised in any way.

As I began the work on this book, I never thought that I was diving into a sea of information. The more I dived, the more pearls I collected. It was an exciting experience because the pearl divers who accompanied me were mostly *nāgasvaram* artists from the age group of twenty-five to eighty-five or *nāgasvaram* music buffs.

Another interesting factor in the study process was that most of the artists are from Tanjavur and Mayavaram pockets. Mayavaram being my ancestral home made it more challenging. The other name for Mayavaram is

Mayiladuthurai — "the banks where peacocks dance". How appropriate for a place where probably peacocks danced to *nāgasvaram* notes on the banks of Kāverī and her tributaries! It was a town where, some decades ago, even a layman could identify a *rāga* and give the correct time.

While speaking to people from different walks of life in and around Tanjavur temples and temples around Mayavaram, I could realize that they all have many comments, suggestions, grievances, requests, etc. and I am placing them on record here for the readers.

- *Nāgasvaram* should be given its due credit and the artists due recognition. A very senior artist and a resident of Tanjavur felt that in those days when Tanjavur was called the "Granary and Food Bowl of the South", there was a lot of *nāgasvaram* music in the temple, almost non-stop.
- The all-pervading music in the air caused abundant rainfall, Kāverī was full with water and with the music always in the air there was always bountiful paddy and prosperity all around.
- Nowadays with many temples cutting down *nāgasvaram* rituals, there is less music or no music. Paddy fields and riverbeds are changing as plots where apartments come up with names like "river-view" or "river side" or "temple view" or "temple side" apartments. These ugly skyscraper apartments even manage to cover the breath-taking view of the beautiful *gopurams*. For common man, to whom the *gopura-darśanam*, was considered as auspicious along with the mellifluous *maṅgala-vādyam* every morning, even from a long distance once upon a time, that is becoming a thing of the past now.
- A temple official expressed his wish on behalf of

devotees, pilgrims and tourists that *nāgasvaram* being the oldest instrument, depicting the socio-culture, history and religion of a nation, should be recognized by the UN as a "heritage" property to be preserved for posterity in the years to come.

It is our duty to preserve our cultural moorings at any cost. There should be sufficient support from the government as the kings in the foregone eras used to encourage and protect the art forms, and the public should also envisage a keen interest in them. And I am confident that the "celestial *nāgasvaram* notes" will never stop; they will continue to echo and re-echo for eternal times.

Some Interesting Snippets

Many interesting incidents have been narrated to us by some of these great *nāgasvaram* stalwarts during their interviews. Some of them are poignant, some hilarious, some unbelievable and some make you wonder whether these artists are really celestial beings like their instruments. Here are a few such incidents to make you ponder over that sometimes truth can be stranger than fiction!

- This incident is believed to have happened during the times of Saint Tyāgarāja in the late 1870s. There was a *nāgasvaram* player by name Dasari (exact dates not available) but tentatively given as 1870s. The artist was playing *nāgasvaram* for the local deity in Thiruvaiyaru Sri Pancandeswarar Temple, while the deity was being taken out in a procession.

  The artist was playing a very popular composition of Saint Tyāgarāja *darini thelusu konti* in the Śuddha Dhanyāsi Rāga. This song interestingly is dedicated to the Goddess Tripurasundarī, the consort of the deity of Thiruvotriyur Tyāgeśa Temple in Chennai.

  Blissful, immersed in devotion and emotion (*bhakti*

and *bhāva*) the artist was oblivious of the composer's presence in the crowd. Once the *kṛti* concluded the saint-composer walked up to the artist and embraced him in appreciation of his rendering. The enthralled crowd went into raptures at this wonderful show of mutual respect and admiration from the great composer to a great artist.

The befitting way by which the saint-composer expressed his admiration to the artist has been compared to Śrī Rāma embracing Śrī Hanumān when he returned from Laṅkā after meeting Sītā.

This story is believed to have taken place in the year 1938 at Myladuthurai Mayooranathaswamy Temple during the Marghazhi month (*thula māsa*) festival between 15 December and 15 January.

- The *nāgasvaram* artist, the great maestro Semponnarkoil Govindaswami Pillai, was playing the Varali Rāga *ālāpana* (*rāga* in detail) to the deity just outside the temple when suddenly the crowd sighted a big cobra on the makeshift *paṇḍāla* (roof) above their heads. While the crowd panicked, the unperturbed artist seems to have said that many a time cobras have appeared when great artists like Sarabha Sastri (flautist) and others played. They will not harm if the music is pure and perfect!
- Here are some interesting stories about Mannargudi Pakkiriswamy Pillai. Once he was invited to play for a wedding and as remuneration, the artist for the three-day affair, received a whopping sum of Rs. 5,000, an elephant, and to and fro tickets in the upper class for twelve accompanying artists. Can you believe this kind of payment somewhere in the early nineteenth century? He named the elephant Sengamalam and

donated her to the Mannargudi Rajagopalaswamy Temple.

He used to travel regularly between Mannargudi and Needamangalam. For this purpose he had engaged the services of a regular horse-cart known as a *jutka*. The *jutka* rider was a Muslim by name Rawooth. When Rawooth's daughter got married Chinna Pakkiri gifted the girl with a *magamalyam* gold chain, but more than that, he performed at the wedding without charging anything.

His instrument with a little golden bell, studded with a diamond, tied to the *mel-anaisu,* is believed to be with the very eminent musicologist B.M. Sundaram now.

- The very popular duo, Keeranur brothers were really not brothers. In fact, they were not even related. A musical programme, by chance, brought them together when they had to perform at a wedding and this incident developed into a relationship that bound them together as brothers till one of them expired. There was total synchronization and harmony between the two in their rendering, and ego had no place in their relationship.
- The late T. Latchappa Pillai's father was attached to the Tyāgarājaswāmi Temple at Thiruvarur. He was an ardent devotee of Tyāgarājaswāmi and would keep uttering "Tyāgeśa" every now and then. Once he was invited to perform at the Nagapatinam Neelayadaksi Temple by a rich landlord who was the patron. He was very particular that Latchappa Pillai's father should perform for that particular festival and offered him Rs. 3,000. That particular day there happened to be a festival at Thiruvarur also. So

despite pleading and cajoling he refused saying that Tyāgeśa was his priority. This happened in the year 1926. When he breathed his last he seems to have uttered Tyāgeśa.

- Nagapatinam Venugopala Pillai was the first to go overseas to perform a *nāgasvaram* concert for a wedding at Malaysia as early as 1920.
- Chidamabaram Vaidyanatha Pillai once performed before the Vanamamalai *maṭha* "Jeer" (head). His performance was so brilliant that the "Jeer" presented him with twenty-five sovereigns in gold asking him to get a golden instrument made. The artist got it made and during his next visit to the *maṭha* he performed playing on the golden *nāgasvaram.*

Sangita Kalanidhi Awardees from the Nāgasvaram Fraternity

The Music Academy is one of the oldest and the most prestigious *sabhās* in Chennai and has completed seventy-five years. The *sabhā* has constituted several awards for musicians. Each year one senior musician from one art stream is chosen by an expert committee to receive this award.

These awards are given every year during the music season in Chennai in December. The highest among these awards is the "Sangita Kalanidhi" award. This awardee also has the honour of presiding over the festival's inauguration and thereafter presides on all days of the festival till Sadas (the concluding date). The award is comprised of a citation, gold medal, etc.

The following *nāgasvaram* artists were awarded the "Sangita Kalanidhi" title:

1. Thiruppamburam Swaminatha Pillai (1953)

2. Thiruvizhimizhalai Subramania Pillai (1956)
3. Thiruvidaimarudur P.S. Veeruswami Pillai (1961)
4. Shaikh Chinnamoulana Sahib (1998)

Valayapatti A.R. Subramaniam Pillai is the only *tavil* artist to have received this award in the year 2009.

Bibliography

Arunachalam, M., *Musical Traditions of Tamil Nadu . . . Festivals of Tamil Nadu.*

Dey, C.R., *The Music and Musical Instruments of Southern India and the Deccan.*

Das, R.K., *Temples of Tamilnadu.*

Dornakal, V.S., *The Music of India.*

Kulendran, N., *Deivaisai.*

Kuppuswamy, Gowri and N. Hariharan, *Readings on Indian Music.*

Natarajan, B., *The City of the Cosmic Dance.*

Ramesan, N., *The Thirumala Temple.*

Sadashivan, K., *Devadasi System in Medieval Tamilnadu.*

Sambamurthy P., *South Indian Music,* vol. 3, Madras: Indian Music Publishing House.

Sampradaya Library, *Music Academy Journal,* Newspaper cuttings, Interview transcriptions.

Sita, S., *Tanjavur: As a Seat of Music.*

Sthalapurāṇam, books of several temples mentioned in the book published by the temple authorities.

Sundaram, B.M. (Tamil University), *Alaya Vazhipadugal Alayavazhpattil Isai.*

Tallotte, William, *Temple of Cidambaram.*

Venkitasubramonia Iyer, S., *Religion, Art and Culture.*

fig. 1: Thiruvarur Temple, in the front is the Kamalalayam Tank

fig. 2a: *Ekkalam* at display

fig. 2b: Kumbakoṇam Temple sculpture seen with *ekkalam*

fig. 3: T. Latchappa Pillai with *mukha-vīṇā*

figs. 4: Tanjavur Temple

fig. 5: Inscription on stone (Tanjavur Temple)

fig. 6: Shri T. Latchappa Pillai with ivory *nāgasvaram* gifted by Rājā Rāja Chozha.

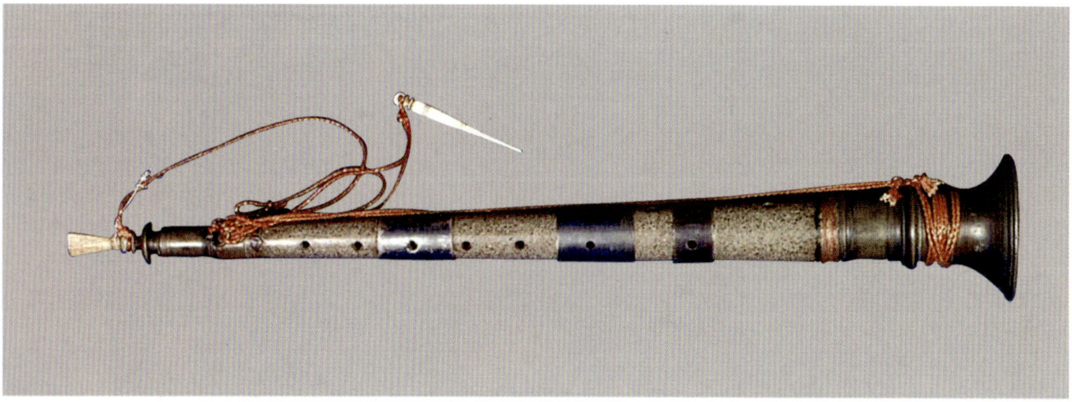

fig. 7: Stone *nāgasvaram* at Kumbakoṇam Ādi Kumbeśvara Temple

fig. 8: Semponnarkoil Temple

fig. 9: T. Latchappa Pillai with the *bāri*

fig. 10: Making of *nāgasvaram* at Narasingapettai. Kannan Ācārya at his workshop

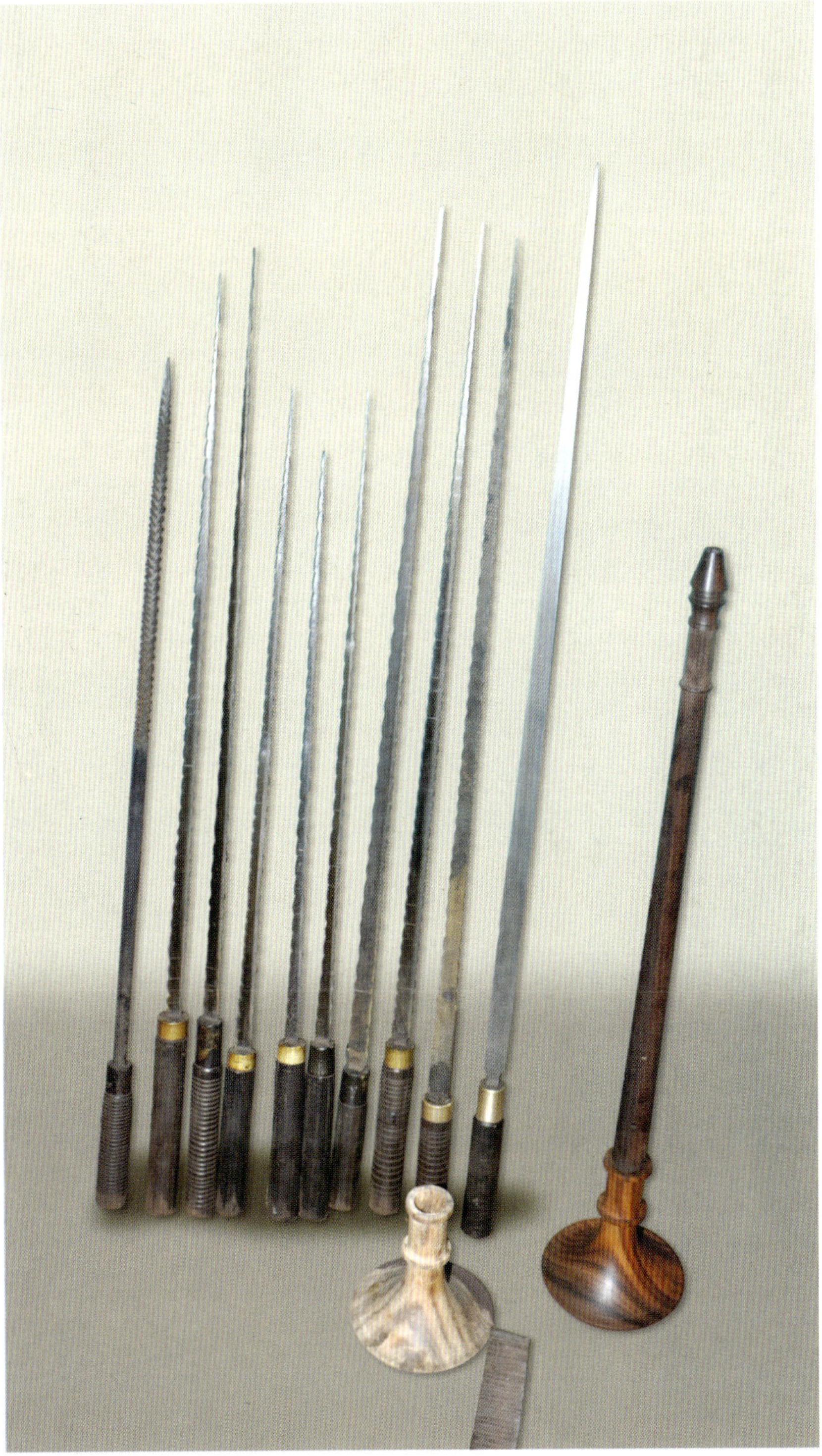

fig. 11: *Nāgasvaram* making in progress

figs.12: Components involved in making of *sīvali*

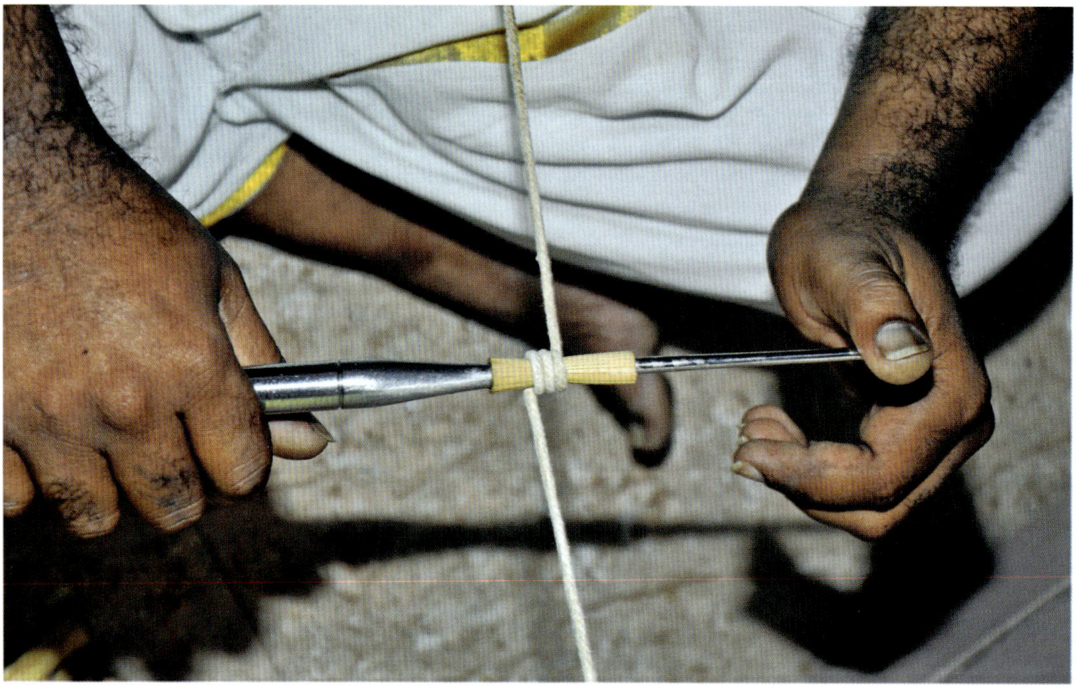

fig. 13: Making of *sīvali* in the final phase

fig. 14: In picture is Shri P.V.K. Sridhar

fig. 15: Types of *nāgasvaram*

fig. 16: Vocalist late T. Sankaran, grandson of Vina Danamal, displaying different *nāgasvaram*s

fig. 17: Mayiladuthurai Temple

fig. 18: Śrī Bālagopāla Temple, Guruvayur.

figs. 19: *Nāgasvaram* students at Thiruvaiyaru Music College

fig. 20: *Nāgasvaram* students at Thiruvaiyaru Music College

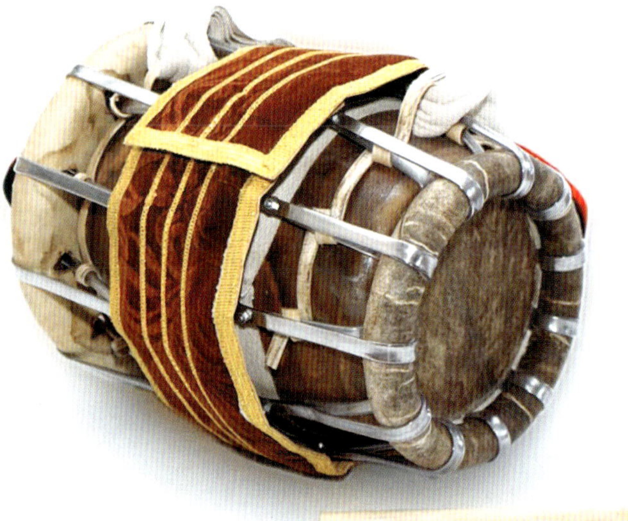

fig. 21: *Tavil*, mother of all *laya* instruments

fig. 22: *Eḍakka*, an occasional accompaniment to *nāgasvaram*

fig. 23: A *pañcamukha vādyam* artist at Thiruvarur

fig. 24: *Śuddha maddalam* accompanies *nāgasvaram* on very special occasions

fig. 25: A scene from *Tyāgarāja ārādhanā* (source: www.thehindu.com)

fig. 26: Mayavaram *tulā* festival procession

fig. 27: Muthuswamy Dikshitar, a great poet and composer

fig. 28: Shri Chidambaram Radhakrishna Pillai playing in Chidambaram Temple

fig. 29: *Nāgasvaram* artists perform at Chidambaram Temple

fig. 30: Śrī Veṅkaṭeśvara Temple, Tirupati

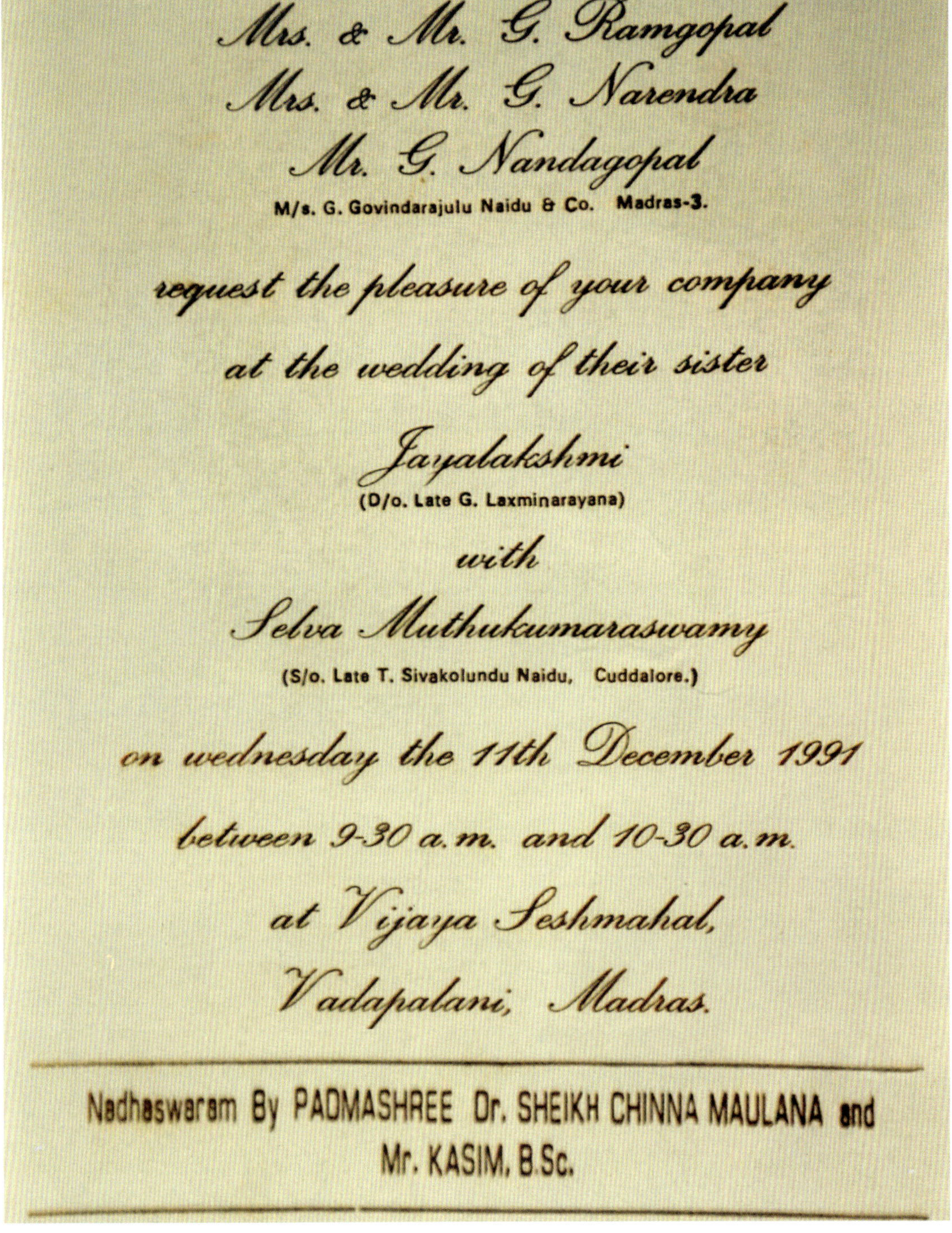
Mrs. & Mr. G. Ramgopal
Mrs. & Mr. G. Narendra
Mr. G. Nandagopal
M/s. G. Govindarajulu Naidu & Co. Madras-3.

request the pleasure of your company
at the wedding of their sister

Jayalakshmi
(D/o. Late G. Laxminarayana)

with

Selva Muthukumaraswamy
(S/o. Late T. Sivakolundu Naidu, Cuddalore.)

on wednesday the 11th December 1991
between 9-30 a.m. and 10-30 a.m.
at Vijaya Seshmahal,
Vadapalani, Madras.

Nadhaswaram By PADMASHREE Dr. SHEIKH CHINNA MAULANA and
Mr. KASIM, B.Sc.

fig. 31: Wedding invitation with *nāgasvaram* artists' names printed on it

fig. 32: *Nāgasvaram* artists play in a wedding procession

fig. 33: Old picture of *nāgasvaram* artists playing in a wedding house

fig. 34: Bhadrachalam Temple

fig. 35: An illuminated Bhadrachalam Temple: a landscape view

fig. 36: Sheikh Shubani and his wife Kaleeshabibi

fig. 37: Late Sheikh Chinnamoulana Sahib

fig. 38: Udupi Śrīkṛṣṇa Temple, Karnataka

fig. 39: Śṛṅgerī Temple, Karnataka

fig. 40: Subramania Temple, Karnataka

fig. 41: Mysore Daśaharā in progress

fig. 42: Śrīkaṇṭeśvara Temple, Nañjanguḍ

fig. 43: K.V. Muniswamappā

fig. 44: Shri Nagaraju

fig. 45: Shri Ramadasappa

fig. 46: Shri D.V. Venkatesaraju

fig. 47: Śrī Pārthasārathi Temple, Ambalapuzha, Kerala

fig. 48: Śrīpadmanābhāswāmi Temple, Trivandrum

fig. 49: Mullakkal Temple, Thiruvizha, Alappuzha, Kerala

fig. 50: The Ambalapuzha brothers — (L-R) Shri K. Sankaranarayana Panicker, Shri K. Gopalakrishna Panicker and Shri K. Ramakrishna Panicker

fig. 51: *Ananta Śayana*: Śrīpadmanabhāswāmi Temple, Trivandrum

fig. 52: Chidambaram Radhakrishna Pillai (*sampradāya* archives)

fig. 53: One of the Kiranur brothers: Chinnathambi Pillai

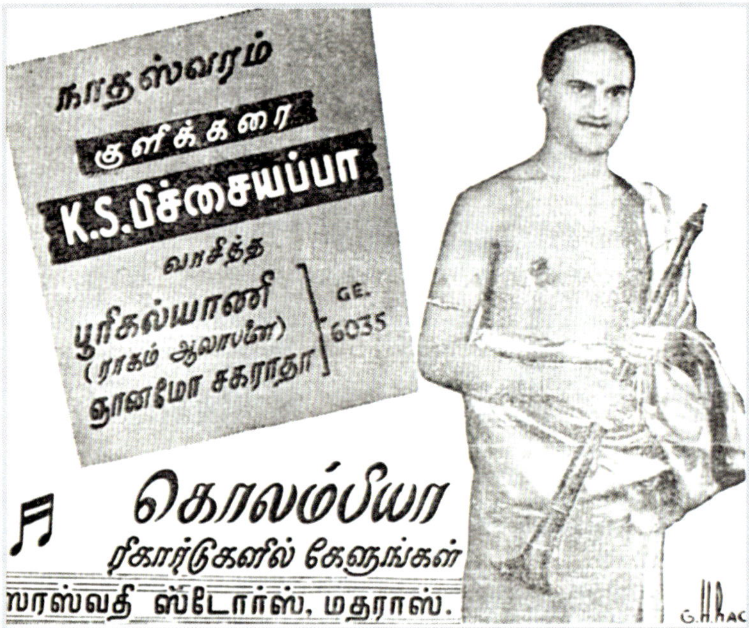

fig. 54: Old gramophone cover of Kuzhikarai Pitchappa Pillai

fig. 55: Kuzhikarai Pitchappa Pillai

fig. 56: Mannargudi Chinna Pakkiri Pillai with his *nāgasvaram*

fig. 57: Semponnarkoil Ramaswamy Pillai

fig. 58: Semponnarkoil brothers at a young age: (L-R) S.R. Sambandam and S.R. Rajanna

fig. 59: Late T.R. Rajarathnam Pillai

fig. 60: An auditorium dedicated to the memory of legend late T.R. Rajarathnam Pillai in Chennai

fig. 61: Thiruvengadu Subramania Pillai

fig. 62: Sri Sivakozhundu Pillai

fig. 63: Shri Venugopala Pillai

fig. 64: Late Thirucherai Shri Subramania Pillai with his students at Tenali, Andhra Pradesh

fig. 65: Thirukazhukunram Temple near Chennai

fig. 66: Sculpture in Thirukazhukunram Temple

fig. 67: Late Thirucherai Sri Sivasubramania Pillai

fig. 68: An artist playing *tālam*

fig. 69: Silver Jubilee picture of Music Academy (many eminent *nāgasvaram* players seen in the photo)

fig. 70: Late Sri Sivasubramania pillai with students at Tenali

fig. 71: Students learning *tavil*

fig. 72: Sri Kannan Acharaya, *nāgasvaram* maker receiving award from Tamil Nadu government

Index